How to Teach in FE with a Hangover

How to Teach in FE with a Hangover

A Practical Survival Guide

Angela Steward

Essential FE Toolkit series

continuum

Continuum International Publishing Group
The Tower Building   80 Maiden Lane, Suite 704
11 York Road   New York
London SE1 7NX   NY 10038

www.continuumbooks.com

British Library Cataloguing-in-Publication Data
A catalogue record for this book is available from the British Library.

ISBN: 9780826495662 (paperback)

Library of Congress Cataloguing-in-Publication Data
Steward, Angela.
    How to teach in FE with a hangover : a practical survival guide / Angela Steward.
        p. cm. – (Essential FE toolkit)
    Includes bibliographical references and index.
    ISBN-13: 978-0-8264-9566-2 (pbk.)
    ISBN-10: 0-8264-9566-4 (pbk.)
    1. Continuing education–Great Britain. 2. Post-compulsory education–Great Britain. I. Title. II. Series.
    LC5256.G7S847 2007
    374.941–dc22   2007017830

Typeset by YHT Ltd, London
Printed and bound in England by
Antony Rowe Ltd, Chippenham, Witshire

Contents

Acknowledgements

Special thanks to colleagues and students in the FE sector for sharing their experiences so that we may all learn from them.

Dedication

In memory of my mother and father for their love, encouragement and support.

Series foreword

THE ESSENTIAL FE TOOLKIT SERIES

Jill Jameson
Series Editor

*In the autumn of 1974, a young woman newly arrived from Africa
landed in Devon to embark on a new life in England. Having
travelled halfway round the world, she still longed for sunny Zim-
babwe. Not sure what career to follow, she took a part-time job
teaching EFL to Finnish students. Enjoying this, she studied
thereafter for a PGCE at the University of Nottingham in Ted
Wragg's Education Department. After teaching in secondary schools,
she returned to university in Cambridge, and, having graduated,
took a job in ILEA in 1984 in adult education. She loved it: there
was something about adult education that woke her up, made her feel
fully alive, newly aware of all the lifelong learning journeys being
followed by so many students and staff around her. The adult
community centre she worked in was a joyful place for diverse multi-
ethnic communities. Everyone was cared for, including 90 year olds
in wheelchairs, toddlers in the crèche, ESOL refugees, city accountants in business suits and university-level graphic design students.
In her eyes, the centre was an educational ideal, a remarkable place
in which, gradually, everyone was helped to learn to be who they
wanted to be. This was the Chequer Centre, Finsbury, EC1, the
'red house', as her daughter saw it, toddling in from the crèche. And
so began the story of a long interest in further education that was to
last for many years ... why, if they did such good work for so many,
were FE centres so underfunded and unrecognized, so under-
appreciated?*

It is with delight that, 33 years after the above story began, I
write the Foreword to *The Essential FE Toolkit*, Continuum's
new book series of 24 books on further education (FE) for
teachers and college leaders. The idea behind the *Toolkit* is to
provide a comprehensive guide to FE in a series of compact,

readable books. The suite of 24 individual books are gathered together to provide the practitioner with an overall FE toolkit in specialist, fact-filled volumes designed to be easily accessible, written by experts with significant knowledge and experience in their individual fields. All of the authors have in-depth understanding of further education. But – *'Why is further education important? Why does it merit a whole series to be written about it?'* you may ask.

At the Association of Colleges Annual Conference in 2005, in a humorous speech to college principals, John Brennan said that, whereas in 1995 further education was a 'political backwater', by 2005 FE had become 'mainstream'. John recalled that, since 1995, there had been '36 separate government or government-sponsored reports or white papers specifically devoted to the post-16 sector'. In our recent regional research report (2006) for the Learning and Skills Development Agency, my co-author Yvonne Hillier and I noted that it was no longer 'raining policy' in FE, as we had described earlier (Hillier and Jameson 2003): there is now a torrent of new initiatives. We thought, in 2003, that an umbrella would suffice to protect you. We'd now recommend buying a boat to navigate these choppy waters, as it looks as if John Brennan's 'mainstream' FE, combined with a tidal wave of government policies, will soon lead to a flood of new interest in the sector, rather than end anytime soon.

There are good reasons for all this government attention on further education. In 2004/05, student numbers in LSC council-funded further education increased to 4.2 million, total college income was around £6.1 billion, and the average college had an annual turnover of £15 million. Further education has rapidly increased in national significance regarding the need for ever greater achievements in UK education and skills training for millions of learners, providing qualifications and workforce training to feed a UK national economy hungrily in competition with other OECD nations. The 120 recommendations of the Foster Review (2005) therefore in the main encourage colleges to focus their work on vocational skills, social inclusion and achieving academic progress. This series is here to consider all three of these areas and more.

The series is written for teaching practitioners, leaders and managers in the 572 FE/LSC-funded institutions in the UK, including FE colleges, adult education and sixth-form institutions, prison education departments, training and workforce development units, local education authorities and community agencies. The series is also written for PGCE/Cert Ed/City & Guilds Initial and continuing professional development (CPD) teacher trainees in universities in the UK, USA, Canada, Australia, New Zealand and beyond. It will also be of interest to staff in the 600 Jobcentre Plus providers in the UK and to many private training organizations. All may find this series of use and interest in learning about FE educational practice in the 24 different areas of these specialist books from experts in the field.

Our use of this somewhat fuzzy term 'practitioners' includes staff in the FE/LSC-funded sector who engage in professional practice in governance, leadership, management, teaching, training, financial and administration services, student support services, ICT and MIS technical support, librarianship, learning resources, marketing, research and development, nursery and crèche services, community and business support, transport and estates management. It is also intended to include staff in a host of other FE services including work-related training, catering, outreach and specialist health, diagnostic additional learning support, pastoral and religious support for students. Updating staff in professional practice is critically important at a time of such continuing radical policy-driven change, and we are pleased to contribute to this nationally and internationally.

We are also privileged to have an exceptional range of authors writing for the series. Many of our series authors are renowned for their work in further education, having worked in the sector for thirty years or more. Some have received OBE or CBE honours, professorships, fellowships and awards for contributions they have made to further education. All have demonstrated a commitment to FE that makes their books come alive with a kind of wise guidance for the reader. Sometimes this is tinged with world-weariness, sometimes with sympathy, humour or excitement. Sometimes the books are just plain clever or a fascinating read, to guide practitioners of the future who will read these works. Together, the books make up a considerable portfolio of assets for you to take with you through your journeys in further education. We hope the experience of reading the books will be interesting, instructive and pleasurable and that experience gained from them will last, renewed, for many seasons.

It has been wonderful to work with all of the authors and with Continuum's UK Education Publisher, Alexandra Webster, on this series. The exhilarating opportunity of developing such a comprehensive toolkit of books probably comes once in a lifetime, if at all. I am privileged to have had this rare opportunity, and I thank the publishers, authors and other contributors to the series for making these books come to life with their fantastic contributions to FE.

Dr Jill Jameson
Series Editor

Series introduction

In his *Review of Further Education (FE)* published in November 2005, Sir Andrew Foster described the FE sector as 'the neglected middle child' of UK education provision, to categorize its role, sandwiched between the compulsory school sector and higher education. Sir Andrew called for improvements in the image, purpose, leadership and skills focus of the sector (Foster 2005). Being under constant pressure to prove oneself and establish positive changes in image, identity and purpose may not always be comfortable, either for a system as a whole or for individual institutions and lecturers within it. In such circumstances, we may find ourselves seemingly always facing a relentless battle of ongoing tasks and problems. To cap it all, the students for whom all this provision and effort is intended may turn out to be difficult to teach: hard to please on a day-to-day basis, stretching our patience and wearing us ragged as we struggle to face yet another challenging day. Does this begin to sound like a bad headache?

Angela Steward, author of *The Essential FE Toolkit Survival Guide for Lecturers* and the *A–Z of Teaching in FE*, herself a lecturer for many years in further education, comes to the rescue of lecturers and others struggling with various kinds of headaches in FE, whether these are caused by one too many drinks in the pub or by personal and professional stressful situations from which we seek relief. Angela explains the role and importance of the solutions we can find to the 'headaches' facing us daily in the FE system in this amusing, supportive and timely book.

Angela reflects on the ways in which FE lecturers can apply a range of useful, proven techniques, learning theories and practical solutions to cure the 'hangovers' of personal and professional difficulties. She encourages us to look at the boundaries between our personal and professional lives in invigorating new ways, applying gestalt theory and insight learning to break through difficulties and find holistic and positive solutions. For once, in this book, lecturers are in the positive position of having their own needs understood and met, rather than constantly catering relentlessly to other people's needs, like the 'Teacher Man', Frank McCourt, whom Angela quotes in her Introduction to this book.

Angela encourages us to apply helpful remedies from a range of learning theories to cure our professional and personal 'hangovers'. Firstly, she applies behaviourist theories to establish good habits that will benefit us in many ways, by making lifestyle changes informed also by an effective application of cognitive learning theory. She makes connections with social constructivist theory regarding the importance of the collaborative nature of learning through social interaction in positive relationships with others, encouraging lecturers to deal effectively with conflict and conflict resolution, whether this is between individuals or between departments and institutions at wider levels. To improve coping strategies for teaching and learning, Angela promotes the use of humanist learning theories to check on our self-concepts and consider opportunities for growth in a range of dimensions and contexts. Finally, she encourages the development of coping strategies and a positive attitude in promoting new understandings from professional practice and constructive ways of dealing with challenges.

This is a very useful book for FE lecturers faced by 'hangovers' of various kinds, whether these are actual physical headaches or the stressful and challenging professional and personal situations that sometimes hang over us. Angela's sympathetic, direct, warmly human approach, informed by a wide range of intellectually useful contributions from learning theory, encourages us to make the most of and the best from our work as lecturers in further education every single day, regardless of the enormity of the challenges of working in FE. This book is essential reading for hard-pressed lecturers in FE to make your burdens more manageable and enjoyable and I recommend it highly to you.

Dr Jill Jameson
Director of Research
School of Education and Training
University of Greenwich

Introduction:
A 'teach-yourself' book

In this chapter you'll find:

- What's this book about?
- What types of hangovers are dealt with?
- What will you learn from this book?
- What's in this book?
- Now – teach yourself!

What's this book about?

> Facing dozens of teenagers every day brings you down to
> earth. At eight am they don't care how you feel. You think
> of the day ahead: five classes, up to one hundred and seventy-
> five American adolescents; moody, hungry, in love, anxious,
> horny, energetic, challenging. No escape. There they are and
> there you are with your headache, your indigestion, echoes
> of your quarrel with your spouse, lover, landlord, your pain-
> in-the-ass son who wants to be Elvis, who appreciates
> nothing you do for him. You couldn't sleep last night. ...
> They're looking at you. You cannot hide. They're waiting.
> What are we doing today, teacher? (McCourt 2005: 67)

You may have experienced the sinking feeling that Frank
McCourt describes so vividly in his memoir of teaching for
thirty years in New York high schools – *Teacher Man*. Your
students wait for you to start the lesson and panic mounts as you
struggle to pull yourself together and face the session ahead.
Frank McCourt suggests that every class is a forty-minute stand
down, you and them; you're just another teacher and they don't
care about your mood, your headache or your troubles as they

have their own problems and *you're* one of them. His advice is to watch your step, don't make yourself a problem or they'll cut you down. So, he says, you stand and wait as they straggle in from the real world; if you bark and snap, you lose them – they stare, you get the silent treatment, they take their time.

Maybe you've experienced something similar when teaching plumbers, caterers, electricians, beauticians, carpenters, mechanics, IT personnel, accountants, artists and teachers in a further education college in the UK. It's the start of a new week and you feel wretched. You still have a hangover after a weekend on the town and you'd rather be anywhere than facing this class. That's what this book is for; it's to help you deal with the headaches this poses.

Most people's everyday understanding of a 'hangover' is of the unpleasant after-effects of overindulgence – usually drinking far too much alcohol. If you've ever experienced this sort of hangover, you know that it's not much fun. You fall off to sleep with your head spinning and wake up with a thumping headache, dry throat, probably aching all over and generally feeling as sick as a dog. After your first experience of a hangover you know what to expect and usually resolve not to suffer in this way again. Despite this, you can almost bet that every day someone teaching in FE wakes up bad-tempered and wishing that yet again they hadn't had one too many drinks the night before. You can almost bet, too, that they'll be wondering: 'When will I ever learn?'

Of course, if you don't have to go to college and teach, you can pull the duvet over your head and stay in bed as long as possible and hope that you'll be left in peace to recover. When you do finally emerge, you'll probably add a feeling of guilt to all the ghastly physical symptoms as you face the critical looks or verbal rebukes of those around you.

If you do have to face a class that day, you probably drink lots of water when you drag yourself out of bed, have a strong cup of tea or coffee and try to pretend that everything is OK. Every time you move your head you are reminded that you have to live with your hangover and get through the day as best as you can – but you suffer and probably everyone else around you suffers too.

What types of hangovers are dealt with?

A hangover does not just mean the after-effects of alcohol or other substance abuse.

- You may feel sick and guilty as you cope with the after-effects of a failed relationship or the fallout after arguments with family or friends.
- Bereavement may have left you reeling with the after-shock of loss.
- You may have had an accident or a diagnosis of serious illness and wonder whether you'll cope.
- Have you got yourself into real debt and find yourself constantly trying to find ways of managing with the aftermath of money worries?
- Perhaps you are trying to juggle two jobs to pay your way or taking on all the overtime you can get and coping with the exhaustion which is an upshot of all this extra work and worry.
- It may be that your confidence is shattered by unspeakable students or by trying to meet the unreasonable expectations of colleagues or accepting the wounding judgement of inspectors after a classroom observation.

Is there anything you can do to lessen the after-effects of the events that life regularly seems to throw at you? Do you sometimes wonder why all these things happen to you and others, seemingly, cope with the ups and downs and appear to coast through life, whereas you reel and lurch from life's knock-backs.

What will you learn from this book?

My understanding of a 'hangover' is that it has a wider meaning than just the after-effects of overindulgence. It's about survival and coping with feelings remaining from past experiences which cloud your present actions, as well as about over-indulgence. As an FE teacher, you spend a great deal of your time *teaching others* and the argument that I put forward in this book is that perhaps you need to spend a bit more of your time *teaching yourself*! I am suggesting that, as an FE teacher, you can use teaching theories, models and ideas to learn how to deal with personal and professional problems you encounter as a student of 'life'. No one is denying it's tough working in the learning and skills sector – and you may feel sometimes that it drives you to drink! It's easier to teach *others* what to do in tough situations than to think about what you can do to *improve things for yourself.*

This is a 'teach-yourself' book which encourages FE teachers to use the expertise gained from learning how to teach others to teach themselves how to deal with the headaches and realities of college life, and to take the opportunity to think about themselves and their teaching in a new light.

What's in this book?

Not everyone is the same: what helps one person learn may not help another as much. In each chapter, therefore, different learning theories are discussed and practical ways to apply them to your situation are introduced. The book employs a range of approaches, which is more likely to increase your chances of learning, and provides familiar ideas about coping with teaching in FE in a new guise. It is acknowledged that day-to-day you do not necessarily refer to relevant theoretical knowledge when you are teaching. Using the book may make you stop and think about how you can apply theories of teaching and learning for your own benefit. There's plenty to encourage reflection!

Chapter 1 – 'Personal and professional boundaries' – advocates that when things go wrong in your personal life, you have to deal with them in college. Vice versa, when things go wrong in college you have to deal with them in your personal life. If you are committed to your job as an FE teacher, you can't create artificial boundaries around the problems encountered in college and keep them separate from your personal life. Wherever and whenever things go wrong, you just have to deal with them. Being aware of boundaries helps you to start to deal with the realities of living. Chapter 1 provides advice through making a link to the theories of gestalt psychologists – which focus on learning gained from breaking the current boundaries in our environment and then reforming them to include new insights.

Chapter 2 – 'Bad habits and guilt' – discusses the notion that you may prefer to focus on one problem at a time and considers problems in the context of teaching. Problems don't just occur, things don't just happen and you can get stuck in your bad habits and guilt about past actions. Chapter 2 provides advice for dealing with a range of classroom problems through a link to behaviourist theories, such as reinforcement, conditioning, reflex and stimulus-response.

Chapter 3 – 'Wrecked and wretched' – is about getting your head around health matters and lifestyle issues. What are you doing to yourself today that will affect your well-being in the future? Chapter 3 covers things like the importance of diet and exercise and the headaches binge drinking and getting into debt give you. It provides advice through a link to cognitive learning theories which promote the idea that gaining knowledge is a continuous process – not an end product – and looks at how you can use problem solving for your own self-development.

Chapter 4 – 'Rocky relationships' – reveals that when the going gets tough poor communication and a bad temper do not help. When personal and professional relationships fail, how do you cope? Have you thought how others see you? Chapter 4 provides advice through a link to social constructivism theories and discusses how adopting ideas about modelling, self-efficacy and a community of practice could help you deal with conflict and understand the importance of social interaction in learning.

Chapter 5 – 'Coping strategies and better teaching' – discusses experiential learning and what it really means for you. The question is: Do you require sympathy or a shake-up? Chapter 5 provides a summary of tips, advice, guidelines, practical examples and identifies what helps you deal with teaching when you're overwhelmed by college life. The final chapter provides this advice through a link to humanist learning theories which involve reflection on experiences and learning as personal growth.

Now – teach yourself!

If you've ever tried to teach with a hangover, or when coping with the after-effects of a personal crisis, then this 'teach-yourself' book is essential reading for you. Why not start on this 'teach-yourself' process by considering my contention that the way you construct both personal and professional boundaries affects the way you deal with the headaches and realities of life in an FE college. Turn to Chapter 1 and think of it as the first step in the process – a chance to gain insights into how you can achieve harmony in your personal and professional life by breaking boundaries!

1 Personal and professional boundaries

Thinking about the meaning of boundaries

The first chapter explores ideas about personal and professional boundaries. You are probably familiar with the notion that you have, what can only be described as, an invisible area of personal space around you and you feel threatened if someone enters your personal space uninvited, say by intrusive eye contact or inappropriate touch. It is as if there is an imaginary boundary all around you which you use to protect yourself from unwanted contact with others – particularly strangers. Also, to show your respect for them, you don't invade another's personal space uninvited. These boundaries make everyone feel comfortable in a crowd or in an intimate group, such as socializing in the pub or working in a classroom, and identify the extent of an individual's personal territory. However, sometimes people erect similar boundaries around their personal and professional *lives* to protect themselves from unwanted pressures or intrusions that are not necessary or appropriate. It is this particular aspect of boundaries that is the focus of this chapter.

The dictionary defines a boundary as 'that which serves to indicate bounds or limits of anything'. It may be important for any society to indicate what is off limits and put up fences, walls, hedges or barriers to signify this. The boundaries may be to keep you out, such as a national border, or to keep you in, such as a prison wall. Whether you consider a boundary is effective probably depends on which side of the boundary you are. When a boundary is set there is almost inevitably some dispute about whether it is in the right place and how successful it is at doing its job. Property owners ensure that they have something to mark the extent of their possession – but, even here, seemingly trivial arguments between homeowners about the height of conifer hedges as boundary markers can become serious when they lead to court action.

Marking boundaries has been customary for some communities for centuries. An old English tradition of walking the bounds of the parish or manor was carried out to check any infringements by neighbours such as moving boundary markers to include good land, ponds and woods or to exclude the hovels of poor peasants so that they would be someone else's responsibility. Centuries ago, as most of the population was illiterate and few records were kept, the details of the boundaries had to be remembered and passed down from one generation to the next. To make sure of that, it was the custom at each boundary marker to beat children with willows or to bang their heads against the markers to drum the information into them. However, as education improved and better records were kept, rough maps were drawn up which fixed and established the geographical area of the parish or manor. So, it was no longer crucial to remember what the boundary markers were and where they were, in order to pass this information on to the next generation, and these cruel practices gradually died out.

Checking your personal and professional boundaries

Nowadays, personal and professional boundaries exist and it's not always easy to get them right, either. Have a look at the statements in the box below and see if you AGREE or DISAGREE with them. Be honest with yourself!

- When I close the classroom door on a Friday I leave my problems there.
- College work and pleasure certainly don't mix at weekends.
- My weekends are for boozing, clubbing, partying and forgetting college.
- I live for the moment and blow tomorrow.
- I dread Monday mornings and they come around too quickly.
- There's never enough time in college to plan sessions properly.
- I muddle through the week as best I can; I don't ask others for help.
- Students always demand more of me than I'm prepared to give.
- I feel under the weather most of the time and don't enjoy teaching.
- My manager never appreciates what a stressful life I have.

Your responses to the statements will provide you with an initial, brief look at how you currently feel about aspects of your personal life and professional life. If you AGREE with MORE statements than you disagree with, then you may have to consider re-drawing boundaries between your personal and professional life if you want to achieve harmony between them. As I said, it's not always easy to get boundaries right!

It may be that you have erected personal boundaries and created a private world within your own four walls at home where you can choose how to spend your time and who to spend it with. You just want to escape the world of work on Fridays after a busy week. Perhaps you still have lots of college paperwork to do but you just don't feel like staying on and doing it, and so you take it home with every intention of getting it done. But you're tired and all-in and resent having to spend your precious free time on college work. Your pile of work sits where you dumped it all weekend. Every time you pass it, you resent it and try to forget about it.

Then on Monday mornings you have to leave this private space and return to college life where you may be working with colleagues that you feel you're at odds with and teaching students who don't seem to appreciate your efforts to support their learning. If Mondays are a day when you always seem to have to make more of an effort to get to college, then the tendency is to try to keep home and college separate. So what do you do? You push work to the back of your mind at weekends. Maybe you find things to do to distract you. Maybe, you just party and let your hair down and boost yourself with a few too many drinks so that you can forget college over the weekend – and then have a few more so that you can face college again on Monday morning.

Picture this: you arrive at the last minute looking dishevelled, marking not done, papers not sorted and nothing really planned for your sessions and, not surprisingly, you have a terrible day and everything goes wrong. All this just confirms for you what a stressful job you have teaching in an FE college. But, unlike people centuries ago who had boundary markers drummed into their heads so they could remember them, you are not illiterate, you are not uneducated and you do not have to set rigid boundaries around parts of your life and beat yourself up as you struggle to keep them in place. You can look at your world differently.

Looking at boundaries differently

Of course, boundaries also ensure everyone's safety and keep us out of danger. Railings around balconies, fences around school playgrounds and barriers along motorways are all intended to protect us. You are *entitled* to your own private space and time to wind down and relax after a hard week's work. I'm not trying to be a killjoy and suggest you never have a break from college work; but take a closer look at what's going on. If *a student* came to your sessions as ill-prepared as you were that Monday morning with their homework not done, assignments incomplete, looking hung-over, under the weather and not acting a hundred per cent, you would be concerned and probably try to talk to them during the session or suggest a tutorial to discuss what was going on. In other words, you'd be bothered and want to do something about it.

Even in a large group, if a student is acting differently, your attention is drawn to them and you feel you ought to do something. You may be worried about the student's demeanour and, once you've noticed a student in some predicament, you may either feel anxious that you don't quite know what to do or, conversely, keen to remonstrate with them or offer guidance. Whatever your reaction, whenever you're addressing the group, this student seems to draw your attention and disrupt your session and you don't know whether to focus on them and their problem, or focus on getting on with the planned session with the rest of the group.

Connections with gestalt theory

It is possible to relate this experience to the notion of 'figure versus ground' expounded in gestalt theory, which may help to clarify things for you. You've probably seen the typical gestalt image representing a white vase — or is it two black faces in profile? When you first look at the picture you usually just see either a vase or faces, but when you are aware of both images you can switch from one image to the other. If you haven't seen this gestalt image go online and have a look so you've a clearer understanding of what I'm talking about (www. learningandteaching.info/learning/gestalt.htm). There is also another really famous image, which you can view either as a beautiful young lady or a haggard old lady, and you may well have seen this in psychology or educational studies textbooks. It's not usually difficult to find either the young or old face but the interesting thing is that you never see a mixture of both; just one or the other.

Those 'double' images explain a particular way of talking about how experiences are structured in gestalt theory and this addresses the question: Just how does the brain decide which is the image and which is the background? In the example I've used, the 'figure of interest' (as gestalt theorists call it) is the student who's acting worryingly and who stands out against the background of the rest of the student group. The 'figure of interest' catches your attention and you begin to concentrate on it, i.e. you want to know what to do. Once you're aware of it, you can't ignore it. Questions come into your mind such as:

- Why are they acting like that?
- Are they just tired or ill?
- Have they been drinking or taking drugs?
- How shall I approach the student?
- What would be helpful?
- What will their response be?
- Should I tell them off or be nice to them?

These questions help you to *think* about what you need to do, but in the end you have to make 'contact' with the student to *find out* what to do. To set your mind at rest, you have to risk a negative response and engage with the student by discussing the problem so you have a clearer idea about how to resolve it.

Again in gestalt terms, this contact might involve 'action' (in this case a discussion) and 'information' (in this case identifying the problem). In attempting to meet your need to deal with the student in your classroom (the 'environment'), you (the 'human organism') make contact across what is called the 'organism-environment boundary'. In gestalt theory, this 'organism-environment boundary' is where learning occurs. In simple terms, from previous experience you know how sessions generally proceed in the classroom because you've planned them and maybe taught similar ones before, and you also know what to expect in terms of a student's behaviour. So, theoretically, when you encounter something new or unknown in your teaching sessions, such as a student acting differently, you risk contact with it to make sense of it. Again, think of the example

I've used and consider whether, in making contact with a student who appears to have a hangover, you would:

- tell the student off;
- be nice to them.

You don't know precisely what will work and what their reaction will be – so when you do something and approach them, you take a risk. Learning about the student's situation occurs as the 'contact' you make with them mediates between you and the environment and you assimilate new ways of thinking about the problem the student poses in your classroom. After taking a risk and discussing things with the student, your newly assimilated information *breaks* the 'contact boundary' as it extends your knowledge of your environment. You now know what the problem is and have worked out ideas about how to deal with it. You benefit from the new knowledge about the student's predicament and in the process become more aware and adjust your response to the student. You can now make a better judgement about whether to remonstrate with them or offer guidance. Theoretically, the 'contact boundary' then reforms and includes your new knowledge and learning.

Gestalt theory and your problems

You would be prepared to take a risk and spend time dealing with a student's problems, but would you be as prepared to take a risk and look at your own problems so readily? For a start, what about that pile of paperwork that you bring home on Friday to do at the weekend and leave untouched until you pick it up and take it back to college on Monday morning?

I suggest that you can use elements from gestalt theory, which were applied to the problem with the student in the classroom, to try to solve a problem *you* are facing. Are you aware that you're not dealing with things as well as your colleagues? Rather than the new learning being about how to deal with the student, your new learning could be about *yourself* when:

- you are the 'figure of interest';
- you make 'contact' with your problem;
- you question what is going on in your life;
- you 'risk' taking action and doing something;
- you gain new insights about your situation;
- you use your new knowledge to deal with the situation.

It is thought that writing things down can often help you to articulate your problems and to focus your mind on an issue and that is what I suggest you do. Harris (1999) makes a useful link to gestalt theories of learning when he identifies that Heron's (1989) model of four *interdependent* forms of understanding is of especial relevance to gestalt theory. In my view as well, Heron's model (see Table 1: 'Understanding your problem' opposite) may be a useful tool for helping you to focus on any problem that may be worrying you, or that you have to face up to, and also enabling you to think about it logically.

Writing down your understanding of the problem in four different ways as you complete Table 1 could be the first step you take to teach yourself how to avoid that awful 'hangover-feeling' experienced when you arrive at work on a Monday morning feeling jaded and ill-prepared, for whatever reason. As you can see, I've already linked my example to Heron's model in Table 1 so now why don't you have a go at writing down an issue *that concerns you* in the blank box under YOUR EXAMPLE. What are you failing to deal with as well as you would like?

The point of using Heron's model is that it makes you consider your problem from four different perspectives:

1 The first step is that you have to recognize that you have a problem.
2 In the second step you have to visualize the problem and appreciate that there is a pattern to your behaviour.
3 Then you have to identify or devise practical ways to go about tackling it.
4 The last step in this model is making an imaginative leap from your present stressful state to a hassle-free future. Well, that's the theory anyway!

Table 1: Understanding your problem

Heron's model	Explanation of the model
1 Conceptual Understanding	1 An understanding that something is the case – usually expressed as propositions
2 Imaginal Understanding	2 An understanding of configurations, and the way that patterns or sequences structure the field
3 Practical Understanding	3 Knowing how to act and developing some proven skill
4 Experiential Understanding	4 Understanding by encounter, face-to-face with the person, the thing, the event

My example applied to model	Your example
1 College work piles up during the week. Paperwork I regularly take home at weekends never gets done	1
2 I have done this almost every weekend this term and feel bad on Mondays	2
3 I will set aside some time daily in college to do paperwork. If it piles up I will do it at home on Sunday mornings	3
4 Tackling paperwork regularly and starting a new week better prepared is less stressful	4

Insight learning

These four steps reinforce an idea central to gestalt theory, which is that you need to see the problem *as a whole* in order to resolve it. It's pretty obvious that just writing down your problem and listing it under the four steps will not miraculously resolve it. Indeed, Atkinson and Claxton (2000) take issue with such a rational way of dealing with personal and professional problems. Advocating the influence of personal intuition in learning, they question the assumption that personal and professional knowledge is best acquired when you are able to articulate problems and explain what you do and know. Atkinson and Claxton suggest that:

- you act and *only later* try to figure out why you did what you did.
- the importance of being able to express knowledge as words (e.g. articulating it and writing it down) is overestimated.

Nevertheless, in my view, writing down your problem is an initial step which will help you to visualize your problem in a new way and see how all the 'bits' make sense together by getting a whole, more consistent picture. You will be generating knowledge that can help your understanding of your problem. The four steps are not about *analysing* the problem but about looking at the problem *as a whole*. You group together events to understand your problem. If you concentrate only on one bit, say either the amount of paperwork at college, or on how little time you have at home at weekends, nothing gets resolved. The problem is still there. The boundaries between home and work remain.

Kohler, one of the psychologists in the gestalt school, wondered how chimpanzees – our near cousins in the animal kingdom – solved problems (Kohler 1925, 1947). He experimented, and observed chimps put boxes on top of each other to get bananas which were suspended just out of their reach. His contention was that the chimps saw how the whole thing might work and acted spontaneously when they made the imaginative leap to get the bananas by standing on the boxes. The chimps didn't just sit around dreaming about eating the bananas; they envisaged a way of getting to them. The answer to the problem lay in visualizing possible solutions and acting on them spontaneously. From the holistic perspective, Kohler suggested that solutions to problems appear to come abruptly, as by 'a flash of insight' (Jarvis 1997: 63). An important aspect of insight learning is that you have to envisage the benefits your actions will bring about. If the chimps just sat around dreaming about eating the bananas they'd be very hungry by now! They dreamed about eating the bananas – but they also did something to realize the dream. If chimps can work out how to solve a problem, I'm sure you can.

Minton (2005: 224) sums up what distinguishes insight learning for gestalt psychologists:

- the solution is a sudden leap, as if pieces were fitting together.
- once is has been accomplished, it is easier to solve similar problems.
- it leads to permanence in learning – it appears to become part of our way of dealing with the world – and we can transfer that learning to unfamiliar situations in different contexts.

So, if you accept Minton's summary and want to resolve problems using insight learning, you need to look at how you deal with things *as a whole* and not concentrate on *one* aspect only. Writing down the four understandings of your problem in Table 1 means that you can actively make sense of all the factors and this activity will enable you to gain an insight into how you will deal with things in the future, which are bothering you now. Insight learning involves pushing the boundaries of your current knowledge and extending the 'organism–environment' boundary to include the new understanding.

Breaking boundaries

The notion of a 'boundary' is an important one in gestalt theory and breaking boundaries is considered necessary for learning and is a positive factor, not a negative one. It's a little bit like cricket – the best scores come from hitting balls over the boundary of the field of play. To score a 'six' the batsman has to keep his eye on the ball and time the stroke correctly. There's great exhilaration when the ball is hit over the boundary, and to achieve the best score the batsman has to be in control of his action. But remember, not every hit is a 'six'. The batsman takes the risk of getting caught or bowled out when he really strikes out and goes for a high score. Likewise, insight learning involves taking a risk and breaking the boundaries of your current knowledge and redefining the 'organism–environment' boundary.

The batsman's score is related not only to his skill but also to the skill of the bowler and fielders, as the other team on the cricket field are *opponents* and out to stop runs. Do you see others as opponents? Think about it:

- Do you feel your friends or family are always criticizing you?
- Do you feel inundated with marking, preparation and administration?
- Do you feel as if students and colleagues are dumping on you?
- Do you feel cynical about the ability of your managers to run the college and consider them responsible for all the additional paperwork you have to contend with?
- Do you feel unenthusiastic about marking students' work quickly because, in your experience, they don't read your feedback properly anyway.

Learning how to solve workplace problems such as these takes place within an existing context, which in gestalt theory is called a 'field', and inevitably your learning is influenced by this field. If you hold views such as those just described, you would be considered '*field-dependent*', that is you rely on *others* for your success – in the examples above this is 'effective managers' and 'committed students'. If you were in this position, you can see that it would be easier to go down the pub to forget your problems and drown your sorrows, as you convince yourself you can't do anything about them.

To deal with college work more effectively, you need to

become more '*field-independent*', that is take responsibility for your own actions and learning. So if you have a problem with teaching with a hangover and work is piling up all around you and you don't have the energy or enthusiasm to tackle it – you have to make some drastic changes. Focus on *yourself* – not on managers, colleagues, students, friends or family. Ask yourself:

- Why am I doing this to myself?
- Why am I handling things this way?
- What's wrong with my life at the moment?
- What are the alternatives?

The answers to these questions have to be self-generated. No one else can impose them on you. One initial answer you might come up with could be that perhaps students simply do more self-checking of their work and another might be to discuss your workload with your manager. There may be ways of reorganizing your timetable. You need to share your concerns with others. You don't have to do everything yourself – remember the bowler in a cricket match relies on fielders and the wicket keeper to stop runs as well. I think that's enough of this cricket analogy – suffice it to say that your personal and professional life is not a game and others are not opponents. These simple answers, or others that you might come up with, will not address the cause of the problem but will alleviate the immediate pressure so that you can think more clearly.

If you look at your problems in a holistic way, it becomes clear that college work and home life are both affected by each other. Your friends and family suffer when you come home moaning and groaning about work, stressed out or even half-cut. At college, students and staff suffer from the effects of your hangover and lack of preparation. Gestalt theories stress the interrelationship of an individual's needs, but people sometimes make false assumptions about their needs. You can convince yourself that alcohol relaxes you and a good supply of cheap booze is needed to help you wind down. Drinking to blank out problems night after night may seem like a good idea at the time. In the past this may have been OK when only you suffered, e.g. when you were a student, but if you've got others relying on you then it is not OK. If you don't make some changes your students will start to complain when their results get worse. Colleagues will begin to feel bitter when you start taking time off to recover and your marking, record keeping and reports are left undone. Managers may get exasperated and threaten disciplinary measures. At home, those close to you suffer as you miss meals, forget appointments and become argumentative. Family and friends feel let down and a partner may walk out.

Surely you can see that you're not using your college time appropriately when you sit at your desk feeling dreadful, keeping your head down and pretending to work. Work it out – you owe your students that time. If you lose several hours' working time in the week because you've got a hangover, then it's only reasonable to do some catching up on work at home. For example, preparing ahead doesn't just mean doing a lesson plan, it means not staying out till all hours drinking so much that you can't work normally next morning. Face up to things! The only way you'll get out of this muddle is to break the boundaries between college and home. Think of your life as a whole – not split into lots of different parts.

Now – teach yourself!

Have you got to a point where you no longer enjoy teaching in FE? Don't wait until a crisis happens before you do something to change your ways. Here are a few ways to break old patterns:

- The secret of changing your ways is to have a clear picture of how much better life will be when you take a bit more control of it. You must envisage the benefits there'll be from the change.
- Remember, problems – or gaps in knowledge – are an important stimulus for learning.
- Don't expect your drinking pals to support your resolution to change. It's hard to make changes and needs a lot of physical resilience, emotional strength and commitment from you.
- If you don't know where to start, why not talk to someone in college whom you can trust and who seems to

have got it all together. Don't just ask colleagues how they cope, but ask specific questions such as:
How do you deal with a student who has a hangover?
How do you organize your sessions successfully?
How do you get your marking done on time?
How do you do your course evaluations effectively?
How do you record statistics for your course?

- Try to make the pieces of your life fit together more harmoniously by preventing problems arising in the first place by thinking ahead, rather than on worrying how to solve them afterwards.

Gestalt psychologists would encourage you to look at what your behaviour is doing to your life *as a whole*. However, if things have got out of hand it may be too difficult to see a way of working things out and breaking the bounds or limits you set. You may be too bogged down even to want to think about your life. You know you have to do something about this state of affairs, but you don't do it. You may not be a holistic learner but a serialist learner (Jarvis 1997) so if this sounds like you at the moment, it may be better for you to try and tackle one thing at a time. This is the approach that is advocated in Chapter 2. Now take the next step in your 'teach-yourself' venture and read Chapter 2 to see if a different approach would be more helpful.

2 Bad habits and guilt

Thinking about different types of hangover

Just how perverse can learning theories be? In Chapter 1 you read that, according to gestalt theories, the secret of successful learning about how to teach in FE with a hangover is to imagine the *future* benefits of actions – and now in this chapter you are going to read about behaviourist theories that say it's *past* experiences that make all the difference. How perverse is that? No wonder students switch off at any mention of theory! If you can't face looking at your life *holistically* as recommended in the first chapter, then perhaps this chapter might be more up your street as in the chapter it's suggested that sometimes it helps to focus on *one* problem at a time and put all your energy into trying to deal with it. Not everyone's teaching is affected by hangovers from excessive drinking or overindulgence. However, I suspect that for many of you bad habits and guilt about past actions create similar symptoms, just like a bad hangover, that need addressing before they get out of hand and undermine you in the classroom.

Two strands are threaded through this chapter. The first

concerns why you keep on doing something even when you know it's not doing you any good, i.e. it's become a bad habit and you are addicted to the behaviour. This doesn't just mean an addiction to alcohol, drugs – whether prescribed or not – or any other substances. Although this type of addiction is the one that usually springs to mind, you can be addicted to gambling, shopping, dieting or even work. These addictions can cause great disruption and concern in your everyday life. However, debilitating addictions such as these require expert guidance and support and you must seek more appropriate help than this book can possibly provide. More modestly, this chapter aims to highlight the negative impact of bad habits on your teaching in FE, which are as bad as any hangover from a drinking session, and how to overcome them.

The second strand in this chapter concerns the guilt you may experience about past actions, which is often misplaced but, nevertheless, hovers in your thoughts and clouds your present actions. Agonizing over things you did months or even years ago can bring on physical symptoms today, such as stomach upsets and sleepless nights. Maybe it's dwelling on difficulties and worries about the past that creates problems as regrets go round and round in your head and you can't shut them out. The nagging guilt can result in headaches – which again are as bad as any hangover – and that means teaching well becomes difficult.

Life is full of misgivings and disappointments but sometimes they get in the way of achieving all we are capable of and become reasons for not doing something. In this chapter I present some straightforward ways of being aware of bad habits and guilt, and how to deal with the hangovers they create – bit by bit – so they don't stop you achieving all you are capable of or affect the quality of your teaching.

Looking at bad habits

Habits can be good or bad. Good habits can help you manage your life successfully so that you make the most of things, whereas bad habits can do just the opposite. If this is true, why does anyone continue with bad habits when they cause problems at home or at work? Behaviourist psychologists would say that any behaviour is learned and habits are formed when patterns of behaviour are repeated. J.B. Watson is generally credited as the first behaviourist (Hillier 2005) and he argued that the environment is seen as providing stimuli to which individuals develop responses. Examples of stimuli could be questions or particular events. In other words, the environment shapes your behaviour and what you learn is determined by aspects in the environment not by you as an individual learner. In these terms, learning is the result of associations forming between stimuli and responses. This may seem like letting you off the hook completely as far as bad habits go. If the environment shapes your behaviour then you can't be responsible for it! Early behaviourist theories ignored the possibility of *unobservable* thought processes occurring in an individual's mind and it was considered that learning could be adequately explained without referring to an unobservable internal stimulus in the individual. But if this was the case, then everyone would behave in very similar ways, and it's pretty obvious if you look around you that this is not so.

What accounts for the differences? First, what you do depends on your learning from *interaction* with the environment and is not just instinctive. This interaction accounts for some differences in response. The fact that people in identical or similar circumstances display striking differences in the way they attend to stimuli in the environment is partly a matter of 'internal disposition' (Child 1997: 95). To check out this theory, think about the following cases and note your response to them:

- I never refuse a drink even though I know I'm over my limit;
- I can't seem to quit smoking even though I know it's seriously damaging my health;
- I often buy things I can't afford because I really hanker after them and can't live without them;
- I can't resist placing a bet regularly even though I hardly ever win;
- I can't just have one chocolate biscuit – once the packet's open I scoff the lot.

Did you think: 'That's just like me' about any of them? They're all examples of bad habits, some obviously more serious than others. But why do some people seem able to resist the lure of these temptations and others not? Can you identify why you can't break any of these bad habits? Maybe you are lucky and didn't recognize yourself in any of these examples. But can you identify other bad habits you've acquired?

What gives one person pleasure may be a source of displeasure to another person. Take smoking: to some it's enjoyable and eases stress while others consider it a dirty, smelly habit which is bad for your health. It is argued that many differences in behaviour exist between those of you who are extroverts and those who are introverts as your approach to life is very different. Attitudes and prejudices may also affect the extent to which you regard certain events or ideas. It may be that your upbringing has left you feeling that gambling is repugnant and so you walk past the betting shop with no inclination at all to go inside and place a wager. You may not condone having a flutter on the lottery either, which for millions of others is just part of their weekly enjoyment and a bit of fun. It's certainly addictive though and, like me, I expect you know several people who just can't stop playing the lottery every week in case their regular numbers come up and they miss out on the big prize! The point is you get caught up in the behaviour – it becomes a habit and you can't stop.

Connections with behaviourist theories

Continuing to buy a lottery ticket is a brilliant example of operant conditioning. The habit becomes strengthened by the frequency of the stimulus-response pairings. The theory according to B.F. Skinner (http://tip.psychology.org/Skinner. html) is that if responses to a situation are followed by a rewarding state of affairs they will be strengthened and become a *habitual* response to that situation, i.e. they are reinforced and likely to recur. However, as you may well already be thinking by now, there are only a few players who receive the reward of the weekly cash prizes in the lottery draw so that can't be the explanation as to why you carry on buying your lottery ticket week after week without so much as a £10 win. The reason is that you can *emit* responses – they are not just elicited by the environment but they can come from within you through what you think or feel. Reinforcement is still the key – but the reinforcement can be anything that strengthens the desired response, such as a feeling of anticipation as you dream how to spend the millions you will win. Your purchase is driven by your expectation of success – even if it is later dashed when your numbers don't come up. The purchase of the ticket, the anticipation and the flights of fancy about spending your winnings are connected as they are so close, i.e. contiguous, and that is the factor that keeps you doing it – not the later disappointment.

Buying a lottery ticket may not be a bad habit, though, as you can probably afford it, you are contributing to charitable causes and you're doing it voluntarily. It is this latter aspect which connects closely with Skinner's behaviourist theory, which differs from that of his predecessors, in that he studied voluntary behaviours used in operating on the environment (Child 1997). Skinner asserted that your behaviour can produce its own reward or reinforcement after analysing laboratory experiments with all sorts of animals; one experiment he set up involved hungry rats. The rats were placed in what have come to be known as 'Skinner boxes' consisting of levers, which when pressed would cause the release of food pellets. In a confined space, the rat would *unintentionally* press the lever as it ran around the box – and food pellets would appear. After two or three accidental presses the rat would quickly learn to press the lever *intentionally* to get the food pellets. In the same way, the theory intimates that you can act intentionally to get the reward you want.

What you can glean from this theory is that the individual must act, or – as behaviourists would say – operate on the environment, in order to get the reward. Learning can start only when the response is emitted. Therefore, the individual's role in learning is not a passive one but an active one.

The context and bad habits

The second key thing that accounts for differences between people's behaviour is that learning is also governed by the context in which it occurs, i.e. certain kinds of behaviour are more appropriate in some situations than others and you quickly learn to recognize this and act accordingly. Despite the fact that your experiences are unique, there are some things to be found in common with the experiences of other lecturers teaching in the FE sector. In the context of FE teaching, consider the following bad habits that colleagues have shared with me over the years. See if you recognize yourself in any of the examples!

- You regularly find yourself arguing with students when they challenge your teaching style.
- You usually avoid discussions in case the class gets out of hand and you lose control.
- You fudge internal verification (or second marking) as you don't want to fall out with colleagues.
- You automatically exclude students from your sessions if they turn up late.
- You try to arrive at your session as late as possible and pack up as early as possible so you don't get too involved with students.
- You avoid answering students' questions as they arise and tell them to ask them at the end of the session just in case you don't know the answers.

These bad habits are a result of conditioned response. If you experience some form of '*punishment*' when confronted by a particular situation, rather than a reward such as the food pellets the rats received, then you try to avoid the situation when it arises again. If you consider the bad habits described above, the punishment could be attributable to several causes. For example, because in the past you were:

- threatened by students challenging your teaching;
- extremely anxious about discussion being either too noisy or no one contributing;

- verbally attacked by a colleague who didn't agree with your comments;
- disrupted by latecomers who didn't know what was going on and ruined the lesson;
- bombarded by students' concerns about the course and questions about when they'll get their work back which you haven't yet marked;
- made to look foolish when students deliberately asked embarrassing questions.

In these incidents, threats, anxiety and embarrassment are deemed punishments. I am sure that if you were socializing in the pub you wouldn't be too worried about friends questioning you about what's going on in your life and why you do things in a certain way, and probably not even too shattered if someone told a story involving you which raised a laugh. You are relaxed in that context and surrounded by friends. However, especially if you're a newcomer to teaching, similar kinds of questions and jokes don't seem quite the same in the classroom. The context makes the difference. Bad experiences in one teaching session or college situation can leave you fearful that they may recur, which is known as secondary conditioning. This has a detrimental effect on your behaviour in teaching sessions and your spontaneity goes, your confidence diminishes and anxiety takes over as you're constantly on the lookout for things to go wrong. Students soon pick up that you're ill at ease and, although the majority don't usually react adversely, there's always a few who do by:

- having a joke at your expense
- chatting when you're trying to give instructions
- ignoring requests to get on with their work
- coming and going as they please
- calling out and picking holes in your teaching.

It's not surprising that you feel undermined and start dreading particular sessions or groups.

Overcoming bad habits

You have read about how habits are shaped – but if they're bad habits, such as the ones lecturers have shared above, what you really need to do is to modify them or get rid of them. How can behaviourist theory help you here? As the individual's role in learning must be an active one you have to think about what you can *actively do* to change your behaviour. Behaviourist theory suggests that if you stop pairing the previous feelings of being threatened, embarrassed and undermined with your current teaching activities the anxiety will eventually cease. In my view, it is extremely difficult to separate the feelings from the actions, and may even be impossible. Although fear of failure might be regarded as a powerful unconditioned response, it is probably the result of much more complex acquired reactions than can be explained just by conditioning (Child 1997). My advice would be that, rather than concentrate on trying to change your bad habits in teaching, you try to concentrate on *establishing good habits* in the classroom or workshop. Ideas to establish good habits and to overcome the bad habits exhibited in the examples I've used above might be to:

- Set aside time at the end of each session to review with students how the lesson went and try to establish an ongoing dialogue about teaching and learning.
- Build up to group discussions gradually by starting off with pairs discussing a specific issue or question. Later on pairs can share ideas in groups of four. Then if this works, groups of eight, etc., discussing more open questions.
- Talk to colleagues about your internal verification (second marking) decisions if they are controversial to give them a chance to explain their initial decision before you submit your report. Remember, it's not a sin to change your mind.
- Establish positive routines for lateness, e.g. students come in without talking and join the group. You speak to them about lateness only at the end of the session when you can express your displeasure that they're missing important topics, while still being fair and reasonable.

- Plan marking time into your timetable and don't make promises to return work by impossible deadlines. If students know the return date they won't hassle you so much in the meantime.
- If the questioner is out to intentionally embarrass you, just say something like: 'I don't know the answer. Why don't you do an internet search and find it out?' Treat the question and the questioner casually – then move on quickly.

In the current climate in FE where emphasis is emphatically on the learner, a good thing about behaviourist theories for you as a lecturer trying to break bad habits and change your behaviour is that the role of the teacher is seen as really important. Sometimes you have to take charge and be a bit more directive in the lesson if you want behaviour to change for the better. Sometimes you have to take in hand the behaviour of a few students so that you create an environment where the majority of students can learn. You don't have to feel guilty about taking charge and establishing positive routines. You will be directing the learning process by selecting the stimuli and by reinforcing the approved responses from the students, while discouraging the wrong responses, e.g. students might have to reach a given point in their work before they can have a break. Discuss your expectations with students, praise good work habits and encourage them when they're struggling to do things the right way. You can do something constructive to overcome your bad habits, and you can use behaviourist theories to explain to the Ofsted inspectors why you're doing it. That could be a rewarding experience in itself!

Dealing with guilt

- If only ...
- Why did I ... ?
- Why didn't I ... ?

I'm sure you've all heard yourself saying these things at some point. You could kick yourself for doing something, or saying something, you now regret. Perhaps you hadn't anticipated the fallout from some ill-considered action. Did you say the wrong thing at the wrong time and hurt someone? It may be that you messed up over an important event which has jeopardized your future. I expect most FE teachers have experienced, at some time or another, the feeling of letting down themselves and their students. The guilt that follows such an experience can be extremely painful.

A colleague told me that he'd reprimanded a student for missing a lesson and he really laid into her when she burst into tears saying something like: 'Putting on the waterworks won't work with me; you need to pull yourself together and buck your ideas up.' Only later did he learn that the student had missed his lesson for a hospital appointment where the specialist confirmed a diagnosis of breast cancer. He felt so bad he could hardly bring himself to face the student again and told me that he didn't question other students about their absences for a long time even though he was under pressure from his manager to check on absences and improve attendance rates. He began to question whether he was cut out to be a good lecturer.

Another colleague, a newcomer to the FE sector, confided to me that in her first year of A level teaching she didn't really understand what one part of the curriculum meant. She kept meaning to ask a colleague or contact the examination board to find out – but never got round to it. The topic came up as a compulsory question in the examination and students came out of the examination room really concerned about their answers and worried how their final grade would be affected. Inevitably, their results were not up to the levels predicted. Colleagues put the poor results down to the inexperience of the lecturer but she didn't see her omission as inexperience and felt guilty that she knew there was a problem but hadn't done anything about it. She knew as well that the results would affect the students' future prospects and carried the burden of this episode around for a long time.

Another colleague confided in me that a couple of years ago she 'mislaid' some students' work. Racking her brain she realized that she'd probably put it in the rubbish bin! The marking was in a supermarket carrier bag which she left in her kitchen and she thought the only answer could be that she picked it up with other rubbish and put it in the bin by mistake. It's the sort of thing that could happen to anybody – but she felt she couldn't admit this as it would make her look so stupid. Instead she told the students the work had to go off to the examination board and – as if this wasn't bad enough – she later prepared a result sheet of imaginary marks which the board had supposedly sent. Having dug herself into this hole, this lecturer felt incapable of extricating herself without losing face. But she suffered. She worried that her guilty secret would be uncovered and knew she had let down herself and her students really badly.

Guilt about past actions – whether innocent or deliberate – can be destructive. Going over past actions in your head and replaying distressing or embarrassing incidents reinforces the regrets and self-doubt ensues. Hillier (2005: 20) suggests that reflecting on your failings as an FE teacher can mean you end up 'racked with guilt'. If you focus on the things that have gone wrong all the time you just end up by blaming yourself – rather than working out how to change things. In his advice for teachers, Moore (2000: 141) recommends that, although emotions like guilt should not be denied, experiences need to be worked through and addressed sooner rather than later as 'regret and self-pity . . . will not, in the end, make things better in future'. Guilt can undermine your good intentions and lead to lack of self-esteem. Instead of dwelling on what has gone wrong and making yourself ill over it, ask yourself as calmly as possible the following questions:

- What specific strategies can I adopt in my future lessons that will help avoid a repetition of what went wrong last time? (i.e. What positive remedial *action* can I take?)
- What circumstances 'external' to the situation in question might have contributed to the difficulty, and to what extent can an understanding of those circumstances *inform* the future action I take? (Moore 2000: 141)

Through these questions, Moore puts his finger precisely on a way to alleviate guilt and self-blame when he urges that teachers make use of *past* experiences but keep the *future* firmly in mind as this can help to depersonalize situations and make it easier to cope with bad feelings, i.e. you work out what to do in response to past situations and take '*responsibility*' without getting drawn into a discourse of '*blame*'.

Now – teach yourself!

Behaviourist theories may have lost their popularity when dealing with students in FE colleges and, I admit, they do not always fully explain how young people and adults learn. Nevertheless, you can gain a lot from adopting some of the behaviourist ideas to confront your problems and they really help you tackle bad habits and deal with guilt. Avoid negative reinforcement by focusing on failure and punishing yourself. Instead, use positive reinforcement by giving yourself rewards for any success. Learn from your mistakes – don't dwell on them.

- Just as in session planning, the process of setting clear goals or objectives will enable you to work out what is important to you to achieve in life whether it be to sort out your finances, go on a diet or improve a relationship.
- It helps if each step in the learning process is short, so break down the task ahead of you into something you can manage by setting short-term, medium-term and long-term goals, e.g.
  By the end of this week, I will . . .
  By the end of this term, I will . . .
  By the end of this academic year, I will . . .
- Identify why you want to change something and how you can best help yourself to achieve the goal. Keep in mind that you can't change other people, only yourself.
- In a similar way to the process of evaluating a session, identify how you will know that you have achieved the goal or objectives you set, i.e. how you will exhibit the changes in your daily life and how others will be able to observe them. Will your bank balance have improved, your weight decreased or your constant criticism reduced?
- Be realistic about what you can achieve and are able to do, take one step at a time and modify your goals if necessary.
- Remember, it's not what you *can do* but what you *actually*

do that counts. You need to practise – new behaviours or skills in the classroom are not acquired without practice.

• Be kind and understanding to yourself – just as you are to your students when they make a real effort but don't achieve as much as they would like.

It is recognized that the effect of rewards and punishments is complicated by learning processes that are more than a reflex action. Some problems do need more thinking about – they may not be solved simply by setting out objectives one, two, three and four. For example, lifestyle and health problems may need a lot more thinking about. So, Chapter 3 focuses on how cognitive learning theories can help you cope with more troublesome 'hangovers'. Do yourself a favour and read it now!

3 Wrecked and wretched

In this chapter you'll find:

- Thinking about how you get wrecked and wretched
- Looking at your lifestyle
- Connections with cognitive learning theories
- Dealing with health issues
- Challenging life events
- Now – teach yourself!

Thinking about how you get wrecked and wretched

In the last chapter, there was a focus on how negative behaviour affects your teaching and ideas were presented for making changes in dealing with the consequences in the classroom or workshop. In this chapter there will be a focus on your lifestyle and life events and ways to overcome feelings of being wrecked and wretched because of what you mistakenly do, or misguidedly don't do, as you go about your daily business either teaching in FE or in life more generally.

This is not the place for a postmodern debate about why one lifestyle is favoured over another. Rather, the purpose of this chapter is to urge you to be open-minded when considering how you could do things differently and take personal responsibility for any actions. In Chapter 3 you are encouraged to create your own lifestyle, contemplate key life events and decide if you want to change anything. Its focus is about learning to learn and, if you choose to make changes, identifying how to teach yourself to overcome problems in life generally which have a bearing on how effective you are in teaching in FE.

If you could see into the future you would find in a thousand years that humans have evolved into mixed-race giants between six and seven feet tall who live up to 120 years. Curry (2006) puts this educated guess down to improved nutrition and medical science. According to Curry's report, *The Bravo Evolution Report*, which he describes as offering a fun way of looking at evolutionary principles, men will have an athletic appearance and women will have big, clear eyes and glossy hair.

However, if you could look further into the future – say ten thousand years – you would then see the consequences of reliance on technology. The scenario painted is that humans will then look more juvenile, social skills may be lost and there could be health problems due to a dependence on medicine.

Go forward even further to a hundred thousand years from now and Curry's report identifies the possibility of more genetic inequality as humans become more choosy about selecting partners and suggests that the logical outcome would be two subspecies of humans: 'gracile' and 'robust' which could be interpreted as the 'haves' and 'have-nots'. The 'gracile' subspecies would be the 'haves' who are described as intelligent, creative, healthy, slim and tall. In contrast, the 'robust' subspecies would be the 'have-nots' who would be less intelligent, unhealthy, grubby, stocky and short.

Obviously, none of us will be around to see if any of this proves true and obviously no one can precisely predict the future, but Curry's report may provide food for thought as it illustrates ways to contemplate the future of our species and what course evolution might take under various conditions. The moral of the story seems to be that, while science and technology have the potential to create ideal conditions for humans over the next thousand years, there is the possibility of a 'monumental genetic hangover' in one hundred thousand years due to an *over-reliance* on science and technology (Curry 2006). While humans can all benefit from advances in medicine, labour-saving devices, etc., it seems that over-reliance on them will enable human nature to degrade and various subspecies of human might emerge.

Looking at your lifestyle

But, let's be a little more realistic and return to the present. It appears that even today many people may not be that concerned with the *future* consequences of their current actions. Their current actions may provoke a 'monumental hangover' in the future through their over-reliance on supports such as smoking, drinking and junk food. At the present time, when there is a frenzy of concern among policymakers, health professionals and the media about the nation's poor eating habits, lack of exercise, increasing obesity, binge drinking and mounting debt, it seems to me that perhaps there is already a possibility of becoming a nation of 'haves' and 'have-nots'. The 'have-nots', who are described as unhealthy and grubby, would be the ones suffering from a monumental hangover and their way of life may leave them feeling wrecked and wretched and certainly not enjoying their teaching in FE.

For now, just focus on your own lifespan and look at your own lifestyle. Perhaps, you may be, wittingly or unwittingly, allowing your physique to degrade through your choice of lifestyle! Concentrate on what you might, or more significantly what you might not, be doing currently that may have consequences for you in the future. Let's find out what your lifestyle is currently like. Questioning yourself about what you choose to do should enable you to think about how you currently choose to live. Are you:

- Exercising regularly?
- Watching what you eat?
- Controlling your drinking?
- Giving up smoking?
- Restraining your spending?
- Using your time well?
- Relaxing enough?

The right answer would obviously be 'Yes' to all the above. Therefore, if you answered 'No' to any of the above it would be the wrong answer – but you'll have to read on to find out why that's not such a bad thing and why a wrong answer is significant and just as informative as a right one!

A lifestyle that is easy and fun in the short term may not help you in the long run. I acknowledge that there is a danger in placing too much emphasis on trying to be a perfect person or trying to achieve an ideal physical type. Those suffering from eating disorders and stress-related illnesses are proof of this. These conditions need expert care, treatment and support, whereas this book offers ways for you to 'teach yourself' how to improve when you are reasonably fit and healthy for everyday life. You need to be sensible when making changes in your lifestyle. However, policymakers and health professionals declare that there's plenty of evidence to show that those who do take care of themselves live healthier, happier lives and are more energetic and productive.

How can you be one of those lucky people? Try this: five, five, thirty, thirty-five, thirty-seven, sixty, seventy, seventy-two, one hundred and forty and ten thousand. Have you any idea why I've included this series of numbers here and what they stand for? It's obviously not the winning numbers in the lottery because the number five is repeated and the highest number in the lottery is 49. In fact, they are target numbers which indicate ideal measurements, intake or activity for today's men and women. Have a look at the magic numbers in the table below.

Target number	What it's for	What it means
5	Cholesterol	You should aim for 5 millimoles per litre of blood or below. 70% of cholesterol is 'bad' and most of the remaining 30% is 'good'
5	Fruit and vegetables	You should try to eat 5 portions of fruit or vegetables daily
30	Exercise	Experts recommend at least 30 minutes of exercise daily to keep healthy
35 or 37	Waistline	The safe measurement for women is 35 inches or less and for men it's 37 inches or less

60	Walking	60 minutes of brisk walking a day is recommended for fitness and to keep your weight down
70	Fat intake	70 grams of fat a day is the recommended daily amount
72	Resting pulse	This is the average beats per minute. The normal range is 60–100
140	Blood pressure	A reading of 140/85 or below is normal. Diabetics should aim for 130/80 or below
10,000	Steps	Taking 10,000 steps daily uses up calories and keeps you fit

Did you recognize these numbers or could you guess what they meant? How do you measure up? If you match these numbers then you're doing well.

Don't know how you match up? For a start you can take your own waist measurement. Then look on food labels before you buy to check the fat content of the product. Get yourself a pedometer – you'll probably be pleasantly surprised just how many steps you take in a normal working day going from session to session in different parts of the building, or walking to the far corner of the college campus for a meeting. Next you could check out some of the other numbers with a doctor or nurse at the practice where you're registered. Most practices offer routine 'well man' and 'well woman' clinics which you can attend and get cholesterol and blood pressure checked out. Alternatively, many chemist shops and pharmacies now offer free tests, so have a look around your local area to see if this facility is available.

It seems that it's as much about what we *don't do* as what we do that leaves us wrecked and wretched, so the following sections in this chapter provide ideas for addressing what you let slip in your life. I believe that cognitive learning theories could help you understand yourself better and would encourage you to use your head to develop ways to improve your health and lifestyle and tackle negative life events more constructively. It may all be a fantasy, but I know which type of human I'd rather be – not in one hundred thousand years, but now! The characteristics of the 'gracile' humans, i.e. the 'haves', would suit me fine today. After all, I'm sure you have found that you need to be fit and full of energy to teach in FE today – not wrecked and wretched.

Connections with cognitive learning theories

If you link learning to behaviourism, as was suggested in Chapter 2, you know when learning has taken place because there is an *observable* change in behaviour, whereas cognitive learning theories depict learning as an internal mental process, which is not necessarily or immediately observable. Making sense of new information is all going on in your mind and others can't read your mind – but cognitive learning theories draw inferences from the way you process information inside your head. Cognitive learning theories embrace a range of theories under one umbrella term – from learning as information processing to learning as cognitive development – and include those sometimes termed cognitive constructivism. Cognitive constructivism is also the forerunner of social constructivism and this is addressed in Chapter 4.

So, how can cognitive learning theories, which essentially originated with the work of Jean Piaget in the 1950s, help you teach yourself to deal with the headaches and realities of a modern lifestyle when they come from an era with very different lifestyles and pressures? Also, Piaget studied children to try to understand how they learned and you might question how relevant his theories are to someone currently teaching teenagers and adults in FE.

Before Piaget's time, the majority of teachers had only been interested in the *right* answers in tests, and his great imaginative leap was to look at test performances in a completely new way (Turner 2004: 71). Piaget saw that by paying attention to the *wrong* answers he could gain critical insights into the thought process of children and concluded that wrong answers indicated particular lines of reasoning; in order to teach anybody you need to understand how they think and what they bring to the learning process from their previous learning.

Do you now see why any *wrong* answers to the earlier

questions about your current lifestyle were significant? Wrong answers provide you with information about how you are currently thinking about your lifestyle. So pause and have a think about how you are thinking! Thinking about your thinking, which is called metacognition, enhances your awareness and ability to control cognitive processes and contributes to better management of your own learning.

Therefore, cognitive learning theories are particularly relevant if you're not coming up with the right answers in life and you're struggling with what it all means! Ausubel et al.'s (1978) contribution to cognitive learning theories is the concept of 'meaningful learning' whereby the learner connects new information to information already known and assimilates it into existing frameworks in the mind. If it doesn't fit, you have to change your way of thinking to accommodate the new information and that may not be easy. One lesson you can learn may be to pay attention to what you are doing 'wrong' or what you're not doing and think about why it doesn't fit with the idea of a healthy lifestyle. Suddenly, your negative response to exhortations from policymakers, health professionals and the media to lead a healthier lifestyle may be just the trigger you need to look actively at your lifestyle and motivate you to teach yourself to make changes for the better.

Dealing with health issues

I am sure that you could recite all the health directives that are constantly being presented to us. You've probably heard them so many times that you take them for granted. Things like:

- Don't smoke!
- Moderate your alcohol intake!
- Eat five portions of fruit and vegetables a day!
- Take regular exercise!

If you're feeling good about yourself then you can follow this advice, but the problem is that when you're feeling stressed it all becomes too much. If you're anxious or tense then that's when you long for a cigarette, reach for another drink or have a chocolate bar instead of a proper meal. Go through the audit of health issues in the table below and find out if your stress may be contributing to an unhealthy lifestyle. Just respond 'Yes' or 'No' to each question.

Healthy lifestyle audit
In the morning, do you: • Feel sluggish when you get out of bed? • Need a cigarette to start the day? • Only wake up after a strong coffee or tea to get you going? • Leave home in a rush and later than you should?
During the day, do you: • Feel sleepy and lethargic? • Crave sugary drinks or chocolate snacks? • Miss lunch because you're too busy to stop? • Lose concentration in class from time to time?
In the evening, do you: • Look forward to a few alcoholic drinks after work to unwind? • Regularly slump in front of the television? • Avoid going out because you're tired? • Get a takeaway because you can't be bothered to cook?
At night, do you: • Lie awake for ages before going to sleep? • Wake in the early hours and can't go back to sleep? • Have disturbing dreams or nightmares regularly? • Feel you get less sleep than you need?

If you had an exemplary lifestyle, then 'No' would be your answer to the questions above. However, I expect you've responded 'Yes' to some of the questions. But don't worry – remember the wrong answers are a clue to your lifestyle choices and to understanding where you're at if you apply Piaget's theory to your own situation. Indeed, Bruner (1977) stresses the importance of discovery learning and urges teachers to encourage students to be responsive in class and contribute whatever they are thinking to class discussions – so that's what I'm urging you to do in response to the questions. Be honest!

However, while Bruner not only urges teachers to be receptive to any wrong answers that might result as they can be used to understand how students are thinking, he also urges teachers to deal with them sensitively so as not to undermine students' confidence. He admits that building up students' confidence is not easy – so don't be too harsh on yourself if you've got lots of 'Yes' answers. Why not try to take time out to relax. Do anything you like as long as you enjoy it. Do nothing if that's what you feel like doing. If you can relax, you are more likely to take note of advice about health issues and do something to improve your lifestyle.

A first step is to go back to the 'Healthy lifestyle audit' and look for the section where you give the most 'Yes' answers. Concentrate on trying to make improvements only for that part of the day. In the table below you'll find a few ideas to get you started.

Healthy lifestyle audit: ideas for change
In the morning: • It's pleasant to wake up to music so set the radio or CD to wake you, rather than an alarm. • Set the time a bit earlier so that you have time to wake up slowly and have a relaxing shower. • Try to drink water or juice first thing rather than tea or coffee. • Have a breakfast, however small, and if you really can't stop don't have a cigarette until you've eaten.
During the day: • Take healthy snacks to college. • Keep a bottle of water handy and take regular sips. • Try to stop even for a short while at lunchtime and eat away from your desk and preferably in company with others. • Get the students actively engaged through presentations, team projects, research, etc. That's how they'll develop their skills and it takes the pressure off you.
In the evening: • Don't drink alone at home and ration yourself to one or two nights in the pub – not every night. • Do a household chore every evening, e.g. changing the bed, doing the laundry, shopping, cleaning, so you leave free time at weekends for relaxing, hobbies and sporting activities. • Take the dog for a walk, go to an exercise class with a friend or do some simple exercises at home.

- Plan ahead so you have the ingredients to cook a quick, healthy meal.

At night:
- Try to establish a regular bedtime routine.
- Avoid eating heavy meals in the evening and drink herbal or fruit teas rather than coffee after your evening meal.
- Decorate your bedroom in calming colours and keep it clutter-free and a place to relax.
- Don't socialize until the early hours every weekday if you regularly have to teach at 9am.

There are no correct answers here – some ideas may work for you while others may not. Many of the ideas you will have already come across and they are just common sense. It's worth trying out some ideas to deal with the stress and overcome the lethargy that drains your enthusiasm for teaching in FE, so write out your ideas in the table below.

This is what I plan to try out or change
- In the morning:
- During the day:
- In the evening:
- At night:

Challenging life events

As can be seen from the previous section, health issues have a major influence on your lifestyle and the way that you approach teaching in FE, but they are not the only pressures people have to cope with nowadays. The cost of living can lead you into debt and the strain of living, or the urge to live for the moment and forget your troubles, can result in binge drinking. For more and more people, these two challenging issues affect how you live your life and consequently have an impact on your teaching in FE as well. This section starts by looking at the challenges of debt and is followed by a discussion on binge drinking.

Employees in the FE sector are not the most highly paid. Many are in part-time or sessional posts and have to manage on the hours they can get. Short-term contracts, threats of restructuring with consequent loss of course hours or redundancy all contribute to a climate of uncertainty in colleges about future employment and salary levels. Across the country, people are in more debt than ever before. Every time you turn on your television, pick up a newspaper or a magazine you are urged to spend, spend, spend. However, it's not just reckless spending that means you end up in debt. Most people put debt down to rash shopping sprees, irresponsible use of credit cards, living beyond your means and gambling, but this is not necessarily the case. Students leaving university now accrue debts for fees, loans and living expenses. Homeowners take out bigger mortgages as house prices rise and householders know the cost of utilities and of the weekly shop usually rises year by year rather than decreases. For commuters transport costs go up and for everyone there are increasing taxes and higher interest rates.

It's not surprising that people are in debt, but there is a huge difference between having enough money to pay all your bills at the end of the week or month – even if you're left with little over for treats – and realizing that you haven't. If you haven't, debts soon get out of control. Some people appear happy-go-lucky about running up debts while others worry themselves sick. For most, when you're in debt it's not just a financial issue but an emotional one as well. Worries about debt can cause depression, ruin relationships and impact on every area of your life – including your teaching.

For those of you who are good at budgeting and know exactly where your money is going, it is often difficult to empathize with family, friends and colleagues who get into a muddle with their money. When you've set up standing orders and direct debits to pay regular bills a few days after your salary has been paid into your bank and are good at working out how much you can spend each month and sticking to it, it's difficult to understand why others can't manage to do it. If you're good with money you probably list all your outgoings against your income and make sure the totals tally.

However, if you are one of those people who have neglected to take a hard look at your finances and are unrealistic about what you can afford, you'll find you can't make the figures tally and you feel as if you're back in primary school trying to get your sums right. Maybe you don't even try working out the sums – it's just a matter of trial and error whether you've enough to pay your way in life. If this is the case, then you're really acting like a child by not taking responsibility for your finances.

Bruner argued that children learn from fundamental principles rather than just mastering facts about a subject. So, if your figures don't tally, it's no good blaming your adding up or shouting at the calculator. What you have to grasp is the principle that if your income is less than your spending then you will end up in debt. You have to understand the relationship between earnings and expenditure.

Bruner believed that children's thinking processes developed progressively and identified three stages which he derived from Piaget's developmental stages and which he later linked to a more general theory of learning (Bruner 1966):

- Enactive stage: learning by doing – problem solving through trial and error.
- Iconic stage: learning by means of images and pictures – only able to deal with known experiences and unable to describe afterwards how a problem was solved.
- Symbolic stage: learning by means of words or numbers – able to hypothesize about what might happen and describe ideas that guide problem solving.

There is an assumption in these theories that thinking develops in stages through a series of changes in childhood and then there is stability in adulthood (Hillier 2005). That would suggest that adults can't easily learn to change their ways. But you can't use that as an excuse as, unlike Piaget, Bruner did not consider that progress and intellectual development was *inevitably* dependent on age, so his ideas can be applied to the way adults learn. His explanation for this differing view was that cognitive development is not an automatic sequence of events because the individual responds to influences from the environment. So, if you encounter difficulties at the symbolic stage – dealing with numbers and figures – you probably revert to the earlier stages in order to solve a problem, whereas what you *really should be doing* is hypothesize about what might happen if you don't do anything about your debts and look for ways of solving your financial problems.

Jarvis (1997) writes that problem solving is also considered the highest order of learning according to another cognitive learning theorist, Gagné, and recognizes problem-solving as an approach typically used in teaching adults where previous experience is frequently a basis for learning. The important thing to remember is that learning takes place in the solving of problems rather than in the acquisition of knowledge. So engaging in problem solving is a really good way to teach yourself. Have a go at completing the statements below.

The financial problem I would really like to solve is:
I would like to improve my finances by changing:
To achieve this, I will endeavour to:

The second challenging issue to be addressed here is the changing attitude to alcohol which is having alarming consequences for many people. A culture of heavy drinking is becoming more commonplace, and greater affluence and young people living away from home are seen as contributory factors to this trend. A report into the drinking habits of over 17,000 young men and women in twenty-one countries (Dantzer et al. 2006) found that more people could be tagged 'binge drinkers' in the UK than in any other European country. Binge drinking is classed as having four or more units of alcohol in one session at least once a fortnight. Not only can you end up so intoxicated that you don't know what you're doing after binge drinking, you could be storing up considerable health problems later on, such as developing serious liver or heart disease. Another serious consideration for women is that drinking more than three glasses of wine a day is said to raise the risk of breast cancer.

Binge drinking fuels violence and Dantzer et al. (2006) report that both men and women are more likely to get into a brawl after heavy drinking. If you go out on the town just to enjoy a drink and let your hair down, your evening may be blighted by drunks fighting, vomiting and urinating in the street or threatening you.

If you've suffered from a monumental hangover recently, this might be an opportune time to check up on your alcohol consumption before it gets really out of hand. Record every alcoholic drink you consume over a fortnight in the diary below.

Drinking diary	Type of drink	No of alcohol units consumed
Week 1 ● Sunday ● Monday ● Tuesday ● Wednesday ● Thursday ● Friday ● Saturday		
Week 2 ● Sunday ● Monday ● Tuesday ● Wednesday ● Thursday ● Friday ● Saturday		

A reason to take stock of your drinking is that, although not all young people who are heavy drinkers end up heavy drinkers in later life, they are at higher risk later. Whatever your age, it's time to think things over and apply Bruner's four key themes to your own learning and teach yourself to control your drinking:

1 Structure – making connections between things such as the amount you drink and your vomiting and headache.
2 Readiness for learning – being willing to make changes in your drinking habits.
3 Intuitive and analytical thinking – sensing there's a problem and thinking about how you can make changes.

4   Motives for learning – thinking about the future and the
    trouble that you are storing up for yourself if you don't
    make some changes.

Now – teach yourself!

Cognitive learning theories state that learning starts from where
the learner is, but teaching can lead it by providing challenging
opportunities so the learner can move on from their current
developmental stage. Therefore, if you wish to be successful at
teaching yourself, you have to challenge yourself. If you're
going around college feeling as if you've got a monumental
hangover which is affecting your teaching, then see how my
suggested answers to questions posed at the beginning of the
chapter could be the 'right answers' for you now.

- *Exercise regularly.* Most experts suggest twenty to thirty
  minutes of exercise three to five times a week. Choose
  something you enjoy otherwise you'll soon give up. Here
  are a few ideas. Yoga improves flexibility and muscle tone
  without working up a sweat! Cycling is easier on your
  joints than running and really makes your muscles work if
  you keep up the pace. You can cycle in the fresh air or as
  part of a routine in a gym. A brisk twenty-minute walk
  can be fitted in most days and just requires a pair of
  comfortable shoes. Swimming regularly is fine and aqua
  aerobics can be fun if you're not a good swimmer. T'ai
  chi, an ancient Chinese method of exercise which com-
  bines slow movements with breath work, can improve
  your general well-being. Then there's skipping, skate-
  boarding, skiing, soccer, snowboarding, etc. Challenge
  yourself to increase your activity levels and do 20 minutes'
  exercise every day, whatever you choose to do.
- *Watch what you eat.* The food you eat provides the energy
  required for every function in the body, e.g. breathing,
  digesting, talking and walking. As a teacher in FE, you
  may be interested to know that your brain uses 50 per cent
  of the energy derived from the food you eat and it's even
  more when you are actively engaging your mind! It's

important, therefore, to get the correct balance of foods to sustain your energy level. If you need extra energy because you've a long day ahead, say teaching an evening class after a busy day, giving an important presentation or organizing an open day, make sure that you eat protein, complex carbohydrates, fruit and vegetables the day before. Avoid high-sugar foods, such as canned drinks, sweets and chocolate, as they raise your blood sugar rapidly but deplete your energy reserves just as rapidly and leave you craving more sugary foods to get you going again. It's easier to concentrate if your energy levels are consistent. Challenge yourself to eat healthy foods and avoid fast foods or junk foods, especially if you have a really busy day ahead.

- *Control your drinking.* Watch the size of drinks you pour for yourself at home. If your glasses are large then a couple of glasses of wine could become more than half a bottle. If you're out socializing, have a non-alcoholic drink between each alcoholic one. Have a glass of wine, then the next round order water or fruit juice. In this way you're still being sociable but limiting your alcohol intake. Try cutting down by drinking low-alcohol beers or lagers and you'll be watching your waistline at the same time! Challenge yourself to calculate the health risks you might be storing up for yourself in the future.

- *Give up smoking.* There's an abundance of advice and guidance out there, but you have to be ready to break your habit and give up (www.ash.org.uk).

- *Restrain your spending.* Keep track of your spending and pay for priorities first, e.g. rent, mortgage, taxes, maintenance, etc. If you have debts then you must tackle them at some point, so don't ignore creditors' calls or letters. You have two choices. The first is to cut down on your spending and not to borrow money or run up an overdraft to pay off your debts. The second is to earn more, use any savings or claim benefits if you're entitled. Neither of these choices is easy. Contact the Citizens Advice Bureau who help people sort out problems with debt (http://www.adviceguide.org.uk). Challenge yourself to being happy with what you have.

- *Use your time well.* Pursue goals that give you a sense of achievement. Don't put off something like lesson preparation until the last minute because then it will become a chore as you rush about in a panic. Set aside a couple of hours and you'll be surprised, not only by how much satisfaction you get from researching material and developing attractive resources, but also by the confidence this gives you when you go into your lesson well-prepared. Use a diary meticulously so that you don't have clashes between college work and personal appointments and end up letting people down. Challenge yourself to find out how you can use your time well and contribute to your community in a wider sense than just working and living in it.

- *Relax enough.* Be realistic about what you can fit into a day. If you're feeling tired all the time, lacking energy and feeling irritable then you could be suffering from stress. The body has to work hard to combat physical and emotional stress and this leaves you feeling run-down. Calm down. Do less and resist the urge to fill every minute of the day. The more you can teach yourself about reducing stress in your day-to-day life the better. Make small changes, such as taking regular breaks at work, and modify your lifestyle to make time for your family and friends. Doing what you enjoy – whether it is having coffee with friends, watching a family member in a sports event or going to the cinema – helps you relax. Challenge yourself to make a list of simple, everyday activities you find relaxing and enjoyable and are relatively easy to do – and then do them.

Have you been able to assimilate everything presented in this chapter, or has it been difficult to accommodate these ideas into what you know and do already? I hope you are now aware of the importance of thinking about your thinking and learning about learning through analysing and hypothesizing about your lifestyle. Bruner (1977) believed that learning should serve the future, and the purpose of this chapter was to help you think about your lifestyle and stop storing up trouble for yourself in future. Cognitive learning theories emphasize the cyclical nature of learning and Bruner's notion of a spiral curriculum encourages you to revisit your learning. It sometimes takes time to change and that is the challenge – so keep on trying and make an effort to get back on track if you lose your way. If you're still feeling wrecked and wretched it may be that you are still at a stage when you need the support of others. A good move now would be to read Chapter 4 where there's an emphasis on learning in collaboration with others. You may 'stretch' yourself, you never know!

4 Rocky relationships

In this chapter you'll find:

- Thinking about relationships
- Looking at rocky relationships
- Connections with social constructivism
- Dealing with conflict and conflict resolution
- Now – teach yourself!

Thinking about relationships

Cognitive learning theories, which were explored in Chapter 3, are concerned with how people take in and understand information, which depends on a readiness to learn and the capability of the individual according to their developmental stage. Tests prove a good source of evidence for educational theorists and Piaget studied wrong answers in tests to come to the above conclusion, whereas Vygotsky (1978) noticed that when children were tested on tasks on their own they seldom did as well as when they were tested after working alongside an adult. The adult wasn't necessarily teaching the child but their involvement enabled the child to think or perform more effectively. In short, Vygotsky concluded from this that social interaction was a critical factor which made it possible for learning to take place. The emphasis in this chapter, therefore, is that both learning and development can be seen as primarily social processes. Learning does not just go on in your head but is influenced by the people you encounter and the opportunities presented or available to you.

This implies that relationships with others are an important factor in learning. The dilemma is that not all relationships are positive and relationships often break down rather than blossom. So, if interaction with others is crucial for learning then there could be a problem. Rogers (2002: 103) agrees with this viewpoint and warns that this emphasis on active engagement of the person with their environment requires two-way communication, which he says presents 'a dialectic with all the potential for conflict' and thus the need for conflict resolution. Conflict can be as disquieting as any hangover and can seriously affect your teaching in FE.

Looking at rocky relationships

Your relationships with students are generally in a state of flux. Things seem to be going fine with a particular student one minute and then something happens – of which you're probably unaware – and reason seems to fly out of the window. If there is a personal crisis or some domestic calamity then it's not difficult to be understanding. However, when there seems to be no grounds for the unreasonable behaviour then it's difficult to be rational and your patience is tested. It may be that the student cannot really explain why they acted as they did or talk about what's really troubling them. It may be that they're going through some form of rebellion such as a need to express independence from family and go their own way – whether this means dropping out of college for one student or, for another, struggling to stay on at college despite family objections or peer pressure. Either way, positive communication between you and the student is jeopardized for the time being, which could affect potential opportunities for learning.

Have you ever worked with a group and realized that, as they got to know each other better, you seemed to be losing the plot? Perhaps you have the group for only part of the week and for the rest of the time the students are all on different work placements. For some students the sessions become a place for socializing as much as learning and general banter takes over from purposeful discussion and disrupts your lesson plans. Other students can't get on with their work and become disillusioned. You notice that tasks are left half-done, portfolios are incomplete and projects are not handed in. You start getting anxious about covering the learning programme and resort to threats about increasing their workload and sarcasm about their ability to achieve. Inevitably, this doesn't go down too well and your relationship with the group deteriorates.

Sometimes you feel as if you're in the crossfire when colleagues fall out. One of them feels hard done by and you are at the receiving end as they pounce on you when you're having a coffee and bend your ear with their criticism of another colleague. Your well-earned break is ruined as you listen to a tirade about what's gone on. Then, just as you're crossing the car park on your way home at the end of the day, you bump into the other colleague and hear a completely different side to the story. You feel caught between the two and wonder how the situation will resolve itself and whether they'll ever learn to get on with each other. Your immediate worry centres on how on earth the relationship will be rebuilt so that you will be able to continue to work together and develop the new module you're all timetabled to deliver next term.

You may find yourself at the sharp end of a colleague's rudeness and wonder what you've done to deserve being shouted at all of a sudden. Other lecturers have been subjected to your colleague's sharp tongue and temper but this is the first time you've been at the receiving end. Perhaps you haven't completed a task they requested and, to your embarrassment, everyone in the staff room is privy to an unwarranted lecture about a trivial oversight on your part. You just sit there and take it and when you go off to teach you feel sure that everyone is talking about you behind your back.

Then again, it may be that you're the one that's on the lookout for what's wrong all the time. Are you the one finding fault and pointing out flaws in friends and family? Perhaps you constantly think of ways that *others* might improve:

- Your child could stop arguing and just get on with their homework when you tell them and then they might not be such a failure in school.
- Your partner could be more understanding and do their share rather than rushing off to the sports club and leaving everything to you at weekends.

- Your friend needs to be told that they're always attracted to the wrong type of person and a new relationship is doomed and spells trouble.
- Your neighbour must be made aware that you don't approve of the colour they've painted their house and it isn't right for the style of the property.

Why can't people be more like you? Why don't they do things like you do? There's nothing wrong in wanting to help others to improve things, but when you're constantly making comparisons, identifying imperfections and making uncalled-for suggestions about how others might do things better or differently, you put pressure on your relationships – both personal and professional. It's difficult to build relationships with others when you're busy looking for perfection all the time. Life need not be a contest to see how many faults you can find in others.

Close partnerships change over time as people develop emotionally, and socially, and begin to want different things. These changes may prove stumbling blocks to communication if both of you don't feel the same and you lack the will or energy to try to understand how it feels to be the other person. Why should it always be you who makes an effort to resolve difficulties? Often one person's insecurity or unhappiness is projected onto a partner. Other people have a way of dis-appointing you if they're:

- not as ambitious as you are
- not as demonstrative as you would like
- not as attractive as they once were
- not as keen to share the same interests as you any more
- not as committed to the partnership as you.

All this leaves you feeling unsettled and in need or reassur-ance. Out of the blue, you're suddenly aware how charming and attentive a colleague can be: they understand how you feel and it's easy to share your problems. Soon you're spending time together and find that you enjoy each other's company and get on well together. You're flattered by the attention and can't believe someone makes you feel so light-hearted. Then you

accept an invitation to go out for a drink or a meal and convince yourself and your long-term partner that it's just a 'work
thing'. You know that things have gone beyond a normal
working relationship but you don't want to stop. You start an
affair. After all, your long-term partner doesn't appreciate you,
etc., etc., and you're entitled to a life.

The secret life that an affair involves is initially exciting but
eventually it does mean lies and deceit. You start dreaming of
how things could be different – swapping your nice but boring
long-term partner, making a fresh start. Things start to get
tough now and decisions have to be made and questions have
to be answered:

- How will my current partner react?
- What about the children?
- Is it love or sex?
- Should you dump your long-term partner?

It's difficult to come up with rational and objective answers if
your mind is in turmoil. When commitment to a new person is
on the cards does the affair start to lose its appeal for one or the
other of you? Fred Sedgwick (2005: 37) in a companion book
for schoolteachers, *How to Teach with a Hangover* (Continuum),
calls the passions of sex without love 'exploitation' and suggests
that 'there is a kind of emotional irresponsibility that toys with
the affections of others'. When you're embroiled in ending a
relationship the pain is palpable but as Fred Sedgwick says you
still have to turn up at school and face a class, and do the best
you can. Exploitation and complications in relationships affect
your teaching in FE, especially if the illicit relationship is with a
colleague in college.

Connections with social constructivism

Social constructivism is so-called because it stresses the importance of the role of culture and context for constructing
understandings of your experiences and the collaborative nature
of learning through social interaction. However, although there
are overlaps between cognitive and social learning theories
(which I referred to in Chapter 3), Vygotsky (1978) rejected

purely cognitive learning theories and argued that all learning took place in a social context and through social interaction. These ideas have been developed in various ways by theorists such as Bandura (1977), Bruner (1977), and Lave and Wenger (1991) and this section looks at how a range of social learning theories are relevant to FE teaching and can be adopted to 'teach yourself' about the importance of social relationships in learning.

One of the best known concepts related to social and constructivist learning theories is Vygotsky's 'zone of proximal development'. His theory is that you can solve some problems or develop certain skills *on your own*, but other problems *can't be solved* or skills developed – even with help. In between these two ends of the spectrum are problems and skills that could be solved or performed *with help*. This middle ground is where the 'zone of proximal development' lies and if you work with the help of a more experienced person – whether it is a parent, friend, teacher, student or colleague – you will solve the problem or develop the skills collaboratively and then be able to do these tasks on your own.

If you want to try out this theory in college, you need to be involved in students' learning and be an active participant in learning tasks – you can't just stand at the front and give instructions and expect the group to get on with their work while you deal with your course admin, sort out your paperwork or catch up with your marking. You have to respond to students' queries and provide guidance if they're not clear about what to do. You have to ensure that their understanding of the task ahead is the same as yours. What you mean by a particular phrase or definition may need clarifying before students can really start working on the activities you've set.

When students are confused and down tools the worst thing for their learning is to tell them the answer – even when they are pleading with you to do so! Learning is achieved through solving the problem, so your role is to guide them, not tell them the answer. Students need an opportunity to construct personal interpretations and meanings through active engagement with the problem or materials. What working in the 'zone of proximal development' offers an FE teacher is the chance to help students 'grasp' what is required as you start to prompt them to make links with what they've done before in previous lessons, or what they may have done at work. The skill is to know when to support – and when to withdraw support – so that students can achieve their potential; it's the ability to 'stretch' students – without them breaking down or cracking up under the pressure!

Bandura's (1977) version of social learning theory emphasizes *modelling* the behaviours, reactions and attitudes of others. You observe what others do and form an idea of how they do it, which guides your subsequent behaviour and actions. Although it might seem that this is just what behaviourist theories entail, Bandura also emphasizes that social learning is fundamental as you are more likely to adopt a modelled behaviour if you judge it to be of value to you and you attach importance to the person modelling it, e.g. you are more likely to emulate the behaviour of someone you admire.

Another term that most people associate with Bandura's work is that of *self-efficacy*, which could be thought of as self-confidence in relation to learning. If you display self-efficacy you are more likely to undertake certain activities if you *believe you are capable of performing them successfully* or accomplishing them. If you believe that you will be successful, then you are more likely to be persistent and keep up the effort to achieve your goal. Students often have a strong sense of what they're good at and what they're useless at, which is usually based on previous successes and failures. If yours is one subject where they've already written themselves off, you have to try and do something to redress this negativity and boost their confidence. This doesn't mean lowering standards so that students can succeed by giving them higher marks on their assignments than their work warrants to encourage them, or telling them that it doesn't matter if they don't pass a test or examination. You can build a student's confidence by making it explicit when they've been successful. There are loads of opportunities that occur during lessons. Everyday examples could be when a question is answered correctly, a tricky name spelled accurately, a rule or definition remembered and even when work is completed and handed in on time. Messages such as:

- 'That's exactly right, well done.'
- 'That's brilliant, it's such an unusual spelling.'
- 'You've got a good memory.'
- 'I knew you'd get it done on time, you're a star.'

These messages draw attention to the student's success. It may not seem much to you, but your positive remarks will mean a lot to students if they are genuine. When a student experiences success they are more receptive to your encouragement to persist and feel it's worth putting in the effort. The experience of success encourages them to believe they are capable of being successful again. Your social interaction with students, therefore, plays a crucial role.

If students are switched off it may be because the learning activities in the classroom or workshop are not directly related to their current workplace practice and, therefore, seem theoretical and irrelevant. Even today there is a view of teaching and training as 'knowledge delivery', i.e. the FE teacher is the knowledge source and the target is students who lack that knowledge (Gherardi et al. 1998). If you take this perspective as an FE teacher, your main effort is to get students to acquire knowledge and store it until they need it – or, as Rogers (1996: 106) deprecatingly says, 'the teacher tells the learner what the ignorant learner needs to know'. A characteristic of this knowledge is that it is too generalized and not specific to any organization or company and so does not appear authentic to students who have workplace experience. Lave and Wenger (1991) argue that the reason for this is that learning is 'situated' and normally occurs as a function of the activity, context and culture in which it occurs – so, in this sense, classroom learning is out of context.

However, if you shift your perspective from learning as a process of acquiring and memorizing, you can reinstate the importance of college study and training, especially for vocational students. What you can do is ensure that the knowledge gained by students in the workplace is brought to the classroom. Each week invite one student to identify a workplace problem or practice encountered and use it as a basis for a group activity. Situated learning is usually unintentional and this activity enables the student to make it explicit. This type of college activity also develops collaboration among the group as they share experiences and develop a wider understanding of workplace culture. Problem-based tasks and hands-on projects are other methods that involve collaborative learning. If a small group of students produces a product – whether it is an artefact, presentation, performance or written project – the social relations among the group members change through the shared experience – usually for the better, but not always! The important thing is that students can share the group's success or develop an awareness of how tricky it can be to work with others and how easily they get upset, or how they upset others. Either way, through social interaction in a small group their experience of developing working relationships with others is expanded if you provide an opportunity for students to reflect on this as part of their assignment or project.

Spending time in college developing relevant cognitive tools to support learning, e.g. strategies for portfolio building and ways of presenting witness testimony and evidence from the workplace, enables students to make links between theory and practice as they construct understandings of what is required to achieve their college qualification. Brown et al. (1989) described this as 'cognitive apprenticeship' and if you adopt this term and call the sessions 'workshops', it makes developing such skills seem part of their overall training and so more relevant and acceptable for vocational students.

Another feature of social learning theories is the notion of a *community of practice* which describes the social processes related to carrying out a practice, e.g. carpentry or social work. Brown et al. theorize that practice is shaped through social relations in the workplace and social relations are created around the activities that take place there, i.e. they are interdependent. Thus, a *community of practice* is defined by its members and the way certain things are done, events interpreted and knowledge transmitted. It suggests a group of people who share and develop ties and creates an image of harmony, but Brown et al. depart from this vision of amiable cooperation. Although the 'community' activity provides the means of developing practice there are inevitable conflicts and power struggles between those who have the expert knowledge and those who don't. Knowledge increases through engagement in the practice but the social processes involved may generate disagreement and differences as people fall out over the way things are done and end up at odds with each other. You can see why Brown et al. suggest that instead of placing a focus on the sense of *community*, which most people do, there should be a focus on *practice*!

Dealing with conflict and conflict resolution

Conflict can rear its head at any time through domestic disputes, personal disagreements or professional jealousy. Sometimes conflict is spoken about as if it occurs in a person's mind, while at other times it is referred to as something that others can see and feel. 'Conflict is a state of mind' according to Huczynski and Buchanan (2001: 770) and has to be perceived by all involved to be considered conflict. If one person is not aware – then it's not conflict.

You usually think of conflict as between two people, but it could be between college departments, between a department and the college management or between you and a particular group of students. The way that a college is organized into departments and sections may encourage conflict and power struggles as scarce resources such as funding, time allocation and specialist classrooms or workshops are competed for. Often conflict arises because you value things differently from other people. You may believe your specialist subject makes an important contribution to a course while perhaps your manager may be thinking of replacing it with something else. You may consider a particular qualification is vital within your vocational area whereas your college offers a different one because it gets funding for it. These situations all have the potential for conflict.

Allegiance to subjects, teams and departments makes a difference to how you interpret events and behave towards others. What you pick up from discussions in a meeting and focus on may get you incensed and yet colleagues wonder why you felt you needed to dispute the decisions taken. Just because you work alongside each other doesn't mean you share the same values and interests, but just because you don't agree with a decision doesn't mean you are being deliberately obstructive. It's not a crime to question how a decision came to be made, but often you feel like a criminal if you dare to disagree or argue for a different solution. The longer you work in any college the more you realize it's not just one big, happy family. You may have experienced this when you mentioned a certain person's name to a colleague and it was like a red rag to a bull. There's an ongoing conflict, which is probably about something that happened some time ago and which might not even be about college issues.

If you have the role of a coordinator in college you will probably be only too aware of conflict between colleagues. You may agree, and it seems obvious, that high levels of cooperation are needed when coordinating collaborative projects such as developing a new course, but perhaps you don't realize that assertive behaviour is also required. This is because when you cooperate, you attempt to satisfy *another*'s concerns, whereas when you are assertive you are attempting to satisfy *your own* concerns (Thomas 1976). Obviously as a coordinator your concerns are that others are contributing, that guidelines are adhered to and deadlines met, so it's no use making your priority keeping everyone happy. You can't force anyone to do anything – or change them as people – but you may have to be assertive to complete the task. Your responsibility as coordinator is bringing all the bits together in the right way at the right time, so it's important to try and draw on everyone's ideas and use insights and materials that different people bring. Even then there's a potential for conflict as each person argues their case, or tasks and responsibilities overlap and people tread on each other's toes.

Yet sometimes it's wise to avoid flare-ups, especially if you're aware that disagreements are not about the work in hand – but about some previous, unconnected incident. Let people cool down and make a suggestion such as: 'Let's agree that the schedule is complete and we'll look at the assessment criteria later.' In this way you achieve a temporary compromise and still acknowledge that there is conflict which needs to be resolved if the work is to be finished successfully. Colleagues (and students) are often fixated by being treated fairly, e.g. if they feel someone's getting away with not doing much. Usually you don't need formal written guidelines, but if someone's not pulling their weight perhaps just an email to confirm what they agreed to do, and by when, would remind them of their commitment to the project.

Here are a few hints that may help with conflict resolution:

- don't rush to intervene and smooth over disagreements;
- make the conflict explicit and avoid 'us–them' stereotypes;
- clarify the goals or timeframe everyone agreed to;
- only refer to your manager when really necessary;
- accept each colleague's position is important – but not necessarily equally convincing.

Now – teach yourself!

Common sense and general knowledge are often conveyed in well-known sayings. These proverbs, or adages, are socially constructed and culturally determined and over the years have been regarded as effective and handy ways of giving advice. Proverbs and adages are usually considered to be words of wisdom that have stood the test of time. However, I'm not so sure. What do you think about the following adages and my interpretations?

- *A problem shared is a problem halved!* It seems easy to find answers to some problems while others remain difficult to resolve even when you've given them a lot of thought. A popular idea is that talking about such problems with someone else is always a good thing. It's a widespread idea that you have to 'work through' negative emotions if you want to put a past incident behind you and before you can start afresh. If you accept that feelings are determined by what you think about, then always focusing on negative feelings can only make you feel worse. The more you go over your problems with someone else, the more likely you are to get into a negative spiral that takes you downwards and keeps you down in the dumps – never upwards and happy and in good spirits which is where you want to be. If you really want to be happy, stop focusing on your negative feelings. Notice the little things that have gone well each day and share those with a friend over coffee rather than dwell on your problems.

- *You have to be cruel to be kind!* The way you feel is determined by your thoughts but you don't necessarily have to share the negative thoughts that keep on jumping into your mind. Contrary to what a lot of people think, you don't even have to listen to your own thoughts, let alone disclose them to others. There's no law that says you have to point out faults in others so that they can learn from them. There's certainly no law that says you have to pass on hurtful remarks or draw attention to past mistakes for someone's own good. You don't have to be the person who thinks 'Well, someone's got to do it'. On the one hand, you don't have to be dishonest but, on the other hand, you don't have to devastate someone either by revealing a few 'home truths'. You can just keep your thoughts to yourself.

- *Take me as you find me!* That's great if you're all smiles, but what about if you're in a bad mood? Should someone else have to put up with your nagging and shouting? If you're in a filthy temper don't vent it on others but ask yourself: What am I really feeling? Try to work out what is underneath your mood. Sometimes you say you're angry and express anger when in fact you might be sad or frustrated. If you can actually say to yourself 'I'm feeling sad today because ...', then you can probably check yourself before you fly off the handle again. It would be even better if you could say it to someone else. It might be scary and you make yourself vulnerable, but at least others would know what was going on and be more likely to empathize.

- *Just be yourself!* You can convey a message even if you're not aware of doing anything. Saying nothing, keeping quiet or not responding all convey messages to others, but, unfortunately, the messages received are not always the messages you want to give. You may just be reflecting and not sure what to say, or thinking about something important so you pass someone in the corridor without smiling or acknowledging them. Unintentionally, you convey that you are not interested or someone feels you are ignoring them and being unfriendly. Communication is a two-way process and just being yourself may not communicate what you really want others to know about you. You don't just communicate with words, your tone of voice, posture and gestures express a lot about you – and the other person is receiving the communication even if you don't realize it. It's only by paying attention to the other person that you have any idea at all about what to do or say next. So be aware – if you want to just be yourself make sure what you communicate is what you want others to receive.

Has this made you think differently? You can use your own common sense and wisdom to decide whether or not to agree with me. That's what social constructivism is all about – you create your own interpretation of information received and construct your own meanings from experiences! It's important to set your own standards and make up your own mind about what is appropriate or inappropriate behaviour and act accordingly. What I hope you have learned from this chapter is the importance of social relationships in learning and I would advocate as Boud (1988: 29) does, that *interdependence*, i.e. working with and helping each other, is 'a more mature form of relationship' which places you in the world and interrelating to it rather than being apart from it. These ideas are developed in Chapter 5 so it's important to read on now for more ideas about how to overcome those hangovers. It's the last chapter so your 'teach-yourself' venture is nearly complete.

5 Coping strategies and better teaching

In this chapter you'll find:

- Thinking about FE teachers
- Connections with humanist learning theories
- Looking at motivation
- Checking your self-concept
- Turning experiences into learning
- Straight from the horse's mouth
- Now – teach yourself!

Thinking about FE teachers

Imagine the scene that Tom Sharpe (2005: 1) is describing in his novel *Wilt in Nowhere*. It's the end of an eventful day and Wilt and a colleague from the local FE college are sitting in the garden of the Duck and Dragon with their beers discussing meetings, financial cuts, redundancies and computerized timetabling:

> 'You'd think the one thing a computer would be good at was sorting classes and putting them in the right rooms. All it requires is logic', said Braintree, Head of English.
>
> 'Logic, my foot. Try using logic with Mrs Robbins who won't teach in Room 156 because Laurence Seaforth is next door in 155 and she can't make herself heard for the din his drama class makes. And Seaforth won't move because he's used 155 for ten solid years ...'
>
> 'It's the human factor. I've had the same sort of trouble with Jackson and Ian Wesley. They're supposed to grade the

same exam papers and if Jackson marks a paper high, Wesley invariably says it's lousy. Human factor every time.'

That's the trouble with FE teachers they're human and behave like humans: every one of you reading this is an individual with your own personality and character! The way you behave as an FE teacher is influenced, as with everyone else, by your outlook on life, your temperament and capability. However, these are not the only influences. The situations you face as an FE teacher interact with your personality and also influence your behaviour. Workplace practices and conditions, such as the endless meetings, financial cuts or fear of redundancy which Wilt and Braintree were discussing, all have a bearing on an individual's attitude towards working in the FE sector. Usually, however, it is thought that the most significant factor tends to be 'other people'. Different people alter your behaviour but, vice versa, your behaviour can also alter other people. So, if you're working alongside colleagues who are entrenched in their ways, incompatible, temperamental or just plain awkward, routine jobs like grading examination papers may prove challenging – as the amusing extract from Tom Sharpe's novel plainly illustrates.

The fulfilment you get from teaching in FE is clearly linked to the quality of your work environment, your own disposition and the temperament of FE teachers you work alongside. But FE teachers don't necessarily approach things uniformly, e.g. some of you may be optimists while some are pessimists and the different ways in which you view your work environment affect your attitude towards your teaching and how you perceive and interpret daily events in college and in the classroom. At any given time, different FE teachers are likely to be striving for different things.

This presents a problem for me as an author of this 'teach yourself' book as, if you all have different needs, how can I identify coping strategies that will be relevant to all of you? That's just the sort of dilemma FE teachers meet every day when faced with a group of students. The diversity among FE teachers is as wide as the diversity among students in college with regards to age, upbringing, ethnicity, educational experience, home circumstances, gender, religious belief, social background, etc. I'm sure that every FE teacher who has gone through an initial training course is familiar with the idea that in any group you teach there will always be students with a range of different learning styles, so you have to adopt a range of different teaching styles and learning activities. What you mustn't do is:

- *Label different students as one particular type of learner.* You must try and encourage students to widen their learning styles and not just rely on their preferred learning style but also develop the ones they use less.
- *Ignore the similarities between students' needs.* Although there is pressure to respond to an individual's needs, students have a lot of things in common.
- *Assume you know what students want from your sessions.* You must encourage them to identify their own goals and try to make their own hopes explicit.

As you progress in your teaching career in FE you become more experienced at planning for differentiated learning and ensuring that individual needs are addressed and students given appropriate opportunities to acquire the skills and knowledge they need for their future.

This is a good point to pause and reflect on your own needs for the future and identify your own goals and hopes, especially if you've taken time to read through the previous chapters and go through the 'Now – teach yourself!' sections. Take a look at the assumptions you make about the way you live and work at the moment. Are you still trying to teach with a hangover?

What do you hope for and what goals have you set yourself to achieve during the next year?	

Connections with humanist learning theories

Have you made time to answer the question above and identify your hopes and goals? You will notice that you haven't been asked to identify 'work' goals or 'personal' hopes separately. This is because 'according to humanist insights, learning is a total personality process; life is a learning experience; true education is individual and about personal growth' (Armitage et al. 2003: 78). Humanistic learning theories place an emphasis on the fulfilment of goals which you set for yourself and so you are at the centre of the learning process and the *learning process* is the crucial factor in Roger's (1974) view: what you do to learn is the primary factor and what you choose to learn is secondary.

You may be currently bogged down by your stressful workload, working through a family crisis or caught up in financial difficulties. Remember, all these can produce the same effect as a hangover and leave you feeling your life is in a mess. If you want things to be different, you have to:

- decide to change
- take responsibility for your decision
- make choices
- find ways of achieving them.

Perhaps you've decided that you're fed up with feeling overwhelmed by life and want to be more successful. This may be your goal, but you will learn most from the way that you go about achieving that goal. Here are some coping strategies that bring into play humanistic learning theories:

- *Admit when you're in the wrong.* Accept that you are human and not always right. You can't always be perfect, but sometimes it's difficult to back down, especially if others have always held your opinion in high regard. If you become more open to the views of other people you may learn new ways of doing things. Rogers (1983) urges us to be ourselves and, if you are genuine, then you make it easier for others to offer help and in this way you can grow as a person. You display strength when you ask for help – not weakness.
- *Be enthusiastic about what you do.* If you can throw yourself

into the small tasks as well as the big undertakings, you will get more pleasure from what you do and be more successful in life. Enthusiasm is catching and motivates those around you. The best thing is that it cheers you up and this makes even the most mundane tasks more fun. Life is only as boring as you make it.

- *Listen to others.* If you talk a lot, you are probably not a very good listener. It is really important to pay attention to what other people share with you if you want to be successful. You learn a lot about people around you from listening to what's *important to them*. Allow others time to say what they want before you respond and try not to interrupt. Remember what others tell you and bring it into the conversation when you next meet. This shows respect and helps demonstrate that you listen.

- *Show appreciation for others.* If you accept people and acknowledge what they have done, either for you or others, then you can build up mutual trust. Notice what other people do well and tell them. Others are more willing to help you achieve your goals if they feel that their contribution is valued and their effort is recognized. Give credit where it's due and make a habit of thanking people.

- *Develop rapport with those around you.* If you want to establish good relations with others then it's important to establish good communication and a feeling of trust. This affinity is essential if you, your students and colleagues are going to participate in constructive conversations about work, and friends and family feel that they can talk to you and that you understand their viewpoint and empathize with their position. When others feel they can say things without being put down or ridiculed and feel free to offer their views on matters, then gradually rapport builds up.

Everybody needs to feel they are treated as human beings. If they're not they moan and groan all day about everything and complain about how badly life treats them, and if you're surrounded by such people then it's likely that you'll end up disillusioned and not caring. Whereas, if you are surrounded by people who are enthusiastic and positive, then you are more likely to feel motivated to succeed. Choose who you spend time with carefully.

Looking at motivation

Motivation and Maslow are two words that are firmly linked in FE teachers' minds, probably during their initial training course. Maslow (1942, 1970) was one of the first theorists to attempt to classify human needs and his famous hierarchy identified two things:

- a classification of motivating factors;
- the relationship between these motivating factors.

Although the reliability of Maslow's hierarchy has been questioned because it fails to take account fully of people's individual differences, it does raise FE teachers' awareness of the importance of motivating students as well as how to maintain their motivation.

A key to achieving your goals through 'teaching yourself' is an understanding of what motivates you. Just like your students, you can be motivated by internal factors such as an intrinsic need to please others, or by external factors such as knowing you'll get a pay rise if you achieve a particular qualification. Can you identify what currently motivates you?

- What are your internal motivators?
- What are your external motivators?

It's important to have aspirations but I am sure you have encountered times when you needed to counsel students about how feasible their goals were. You, too, have to be realistic and take into account your individual skills, abilities and knowledge as they all affect how successful you are at achieving your goals and how motivated you remain. The following factors help you to achieve your own goals.

- *Self-confidence.* You need the personal resources to be successful, i.e. you need confidence in your own ability, so assess whether you are willing to spend time acquiring the skills or knowledge necessary to achieve.

- *Choice.* Make sure you really want to achieve the goal or else you may give up when things get tough. Remember, though, nothing worth doing is ever easy.
- *Commitment.* Set yourself 'mini-goals' or steps to keep you motivated and so you can see the progress you've made by breaking down a task into, say, week-by-week targets.
- *Feedback.* You need to know if you're on track to succeed. Share your goals with someone you trust and talk to them about how you're doing. It's important to get confirmation that you're on the right lines and, if necessary, get any errors sorted out.

You can probably see how the coping strategies could be useful to you, but remember that you could also use them as external motivators with your students. The good thing about motivational theories is that they identify a role for the FE teacher. Someone needs you! The FE teacher plays a positive role as an external motivator and your ongoing support may make all the difference when a student is struggling to achieve. So, if *you're* struggling, identify your internal motivators and link up with someone who can be an external motivator. You could start your own learning circle or community of practice!

Checking your self-concept

What I hope you have learned from this 'teach yourself' book, and what Hillier (2005: 80) has already eloquently identified, is that learning draws on many theories and is thus multi-disciplinary, and multi-disciplinary theories 'take account of both the individual as an actor in the world and the world in which the individual lives'.

The first step, therefore, is to consider how you see yourself as an individual in the world. Rogers (1983) imagines an individual's self-concept as a 'two-sided self', and Huczynski and Buchanan (2001: 162) present this as a model which may be a useful device to help you look at the image you have of yourself.

An individual's self-concept: the two-sided self

The way 'I' see myself	The way others see me
What I expect of myself	What others expect of me
The personal self: my perceptions, motives, feelings	The social self: how I appear to others

Table adapted from Huczynski and Buchanan (2001: 162)

The theory of self and the idea of self-concept both deserve a brief examination.

- 'I' is the unique individual – other people encourage you to conform to current values and beliefs but individuals are also capable of adjusting and changing.
- 'Me' is an aspect of self and reveals your attitudes, etc., and enables you to reflect on your own behaviour and 'look' at yourself.
- 'Other' is a set of expectations you believe others have of you.
- 'Self-concept' provides a sense of meaning and consistency in our lives, but is not fixed. If you have an accurate perception of your qualities, abilities, attitudes, etc., then you can be free from tension and capable of changing.

There are lots of theories about 'personality types' and one of the most well-known is the way Eysenck (1973) identifies personality traits. Perhaps a glance at the following table will also help you look at the image you have of yourself.

EXTROVERT	INTROVERT
Activity	Inactivity
Expressiveness	Inhibition
Impulsiveness	Control
Irresponsibility	Responsibility
Practicality	Reflectiveness
Risk-taking	Carefulness
Sociability	Unsociability

EMOTIONALLY UNSTABLE	EMOTIONALLY STABLE
Anxiety	Calm
Guilt	Guilt freedom
Hypochondriasis	Sense of health
Lack of autonomy	Autonomy
Low self-esteem	Self-esteem
Obsessiveness	Casualness
Unhappiness	Happiness

For a bit of fun, make a list of ten words or phrases which describe you as an individual and how you see yourself.

Turning experiences into learning

Let's move on to the second step Hillier (2005) drew attention to, which takes account of the world in which you live:

> The physical world which we inhabit, the built environment which we have made for ourselves, the mental world which we have created as well as the social environment are all elements with which we are bound in a perpetual engagement. (Rogers 2002: 104)

Rogers explains that your *total* environment and your experiences are constantly interacting and you are your experiences, so to speak. According to Maslow's hierarchy, at the core of human personality is the desire to realize one's full potential, but Carl Rogers (1974) asserts that for this to happen you need the right environment. He says it depends on experiencing unconditional positive regard in your environment, i.e. you are accepted and valued, trusted and respected whatever your personality. Humanistic theories represent life as a quest for personal growth and this is achieved by observing and reflecting on your experiences and making sense of them – at the core of learning is searching for meaning in experiences.

However, you don't necessarily learn from every experience, and personal growth doesn't just happen because you've experienced something. Argyris and Schon (1974) identify two kinds of learning from experience:

- *Single-loop learning*. You do something but you don't challenge why and you don't rethink your values or assumptions about what you did. You go on doing what you have been doing in the same old way – so your learning is limited to small changes.
- *Double-loop learning*. Rather than accepting things and working within the limitations this presents, you challenge your assumptions, your beliefs, your routine ways of doing things and your decisions. This type of learning centres on learning how to learn.

Two questions illustrate the difference between these two types of learning. In single-loop learning the question might be:

How can I achieve my goals?

Whereas in double-loop learning the question might be:

Are my goals appropriate?

Can you see how the second question would make you challenge your assumptions about what you are doing and your decisions about what you identify and set as your goals? If you want to learn from life's experiences you have to start to question yourself and confront your beliefs.

From what has been said, it is clear that for learning to take place you have to search actively for meaning in experience, as personal growth requires you to question and critically reflect on what you experience. It's here that I would be failing if I didn't introduce Kolb's (1984) Learning Cycle, which every FE teacher will no doubt recognize from their educational studies. I don't need to draw a picture of this framework of experiential learning here, but just to remind you Kolb advocates that critical reflection on experience is the key strategy in making that experience meaningful and from this reflection you form an opinion, or hypothesis, about the new meaning and then try it out. However, Kolb's Learning Cycle isn't necessarily the answer to all your problems. Even if you've gone through this Learning Cycle of reflection on experience it still doesn't *guarantee* that you won't repeat past mistakes or that everything makes sense and takes on a new meaning. Kolb indicates that there is always conflict and tension in learning, e.g. between reflection and action and concrete happenings and abstract thought. Some problems you face in life may not have answers, however much you reflect on them:

- you can't put the clock back;
- you can't make someone love you;
- you can't bring back someone who's left you;
- you can't cure someone of a serious illness/condition;
- you can't control others' lives.

Schumaker's (1977: 3) philosophical view is that 'difficult circumstances present problems, and it might be said that living means, above all else, dealing with problems'. Some problems may be solved – but you have to accept that others may not have an easy solution. What you can reflect on is that any experience may lead to new challenges to act on as you face up to your problems.

Straight from the horse's mouth

In the Introduction to this book, I explained that a hangover does not just mean the after-effects of alcohol or other substance abuse but could be the result of failed relationships, bereavement, an accident, debts, exhaustion, guilt or humiliating experiences. A whole range of FE teachers have shared with me their ways of dealing with life's hangovers. The following is a selection of their stories which are their interpretations of the experiences they encountered and how they acted to cure their particular version of a hangover.

- When my son was seriously ill, I used to arrive at class and think: As soon as I finish here I'll be on my way to visit him in hospital. Just thinking that got me through and I kept saying to myself only three hours, only two hours, only one hour, etc. I know it sounds awful, but it really helped me with timing my lessons. I was a bit slapdash. I teach art and never worried about how long activities would take or if I didn't get through what was planned and sometimes ran over time and expected the students to stay and finish off work. When I knew I had to get away promptly, it made me start the lessons promptly and get the students involved and working as soon as possible. I began to tell them what was going to happen in the lesson, how long they had to spend on certain things and what they had to do so that the lesson could finish on time. I told them why – and suddenly they seemed more cooperative. I relaxed because I knew I could get away and the students knew where they were – so we had some lovely lessons even though personally for me it was a terrible time and it was constantly on my mind how ill my son was. If I had to put my advice into a few words as you ask, it would be: Don't keep students in the dark and make the most of every minute – don't wish your life away. (Lecturer in Creative Arts)

- When I first started teaching I had an evening class on a Wednesday and it was too much of a rush to go home after my afternoon class. I got into the habit of going to the pub for a sandwich and soon found that I was having one or two beers as well. During a break one evening, I overheard two of my students chatting and one was saying he wasn't coming back after break because it was a waste of time as 'he's drunk, you can smell it on his breath'. They say listeners never hear any good of themselves, and that was a shock. It made me realize how I looked to others – I just hadn't thought of that before and it pulled me up sharp. The answer to your question is that if you want to teach, don't do it with a hangover. If you want to be respected, don't drink a couple of beers before a class. I learned my lesson the hard way. Don't drink and teach! (Lecturer in Management Studies)

- I certainly felt I had a constant hangover when my partner first asked for a divorce. I felt physically sick, didn't really want to do anything and found it a struggle to get to work and had loads of time off. When I did go in it felt as if the students were constantly shouting and being difficult and I went around with a terrible headache most of the time. In my appraisal my manager said, although she understood my circumstances, she was very unhappy with my performance and that I was putting my job under threat. I felt at rock bottom after this and I thought if I lose my job too I've got nothing. I'll be one of life's losers. So I said to myself you'll just have to make your job your life as you've got no partner and no social life. How sad is that. Then a funny thing happened, a colleague had broken his arm and asked if I could give him a lift in to work. That really helped me get to work every day and of course as I began to get more continuity in my lessons the students seemed to settle down. So things got better and I began to enjoy my job again. It's strange, but I felt I shouldn't be enjoying anything when life was so awful, but when the new college year started I thought this is the start of my new life. Corny I know, but I put more effort in and I enjoyed it. I gradually regained my confidence – not just in my teaching but in myself. I even thought I wouldn't be able to do all this if I was still married. What I would say to anyone who's in a similar situation is to treat your job like a good friend, look after it, enjoy it, as you need all the friends you can get in life. (Lecturer in Travel, Tourism and Leisure)

- I've always been a bit shy and quiet but have always got on well in college as I know my industry inside out. I got promotion which involves visiting employers quite a bit and I find this a bit stressful as the travelling is time-consuming and so is meeting new people all the time. I did let things go a bit at work, you know, got a bit behind. One day I got back to work after a meeting with a really important employer and was a bit shattered and just sat at my desk in a bit of a daze really. Suddenly I heard this colleague, who made it very clear he didn't think I should have got my promotion and who is always on my back and on his high horse about something and making my life a misery, shouting really loudly and sarcastically, why didn't I get on with my *'blankety-blank'* work instead of swanning around hobnobbing with employers and sitting there as if I owned the place because he couldn't get on with his job because I spent my time on more important things and why didn't I pull my '*blankety-blank*' finger out. I just turned round and said, and I remember it exactly, 'You are an out and out bully and I'm going to put in an official complaint about you and these people here are my witnesses'. I'd never even thought of this before, and I really had no intention of doing it, and never did, but it did the trick. I'm glad I didn't resort to shouting and swearing as I had imagined I would one day. If your hangovers are because of bullying, my advice is that even a weakling like me can stand up for themselves. (Lecturer in Construction)

Some of the coping strategies might not be what you expected to hear. Nevertheless, the coping strategies worked for them – so perhaps they can work for you. By reflecting on our experiences, 'we can become positive in our search for new understandings of our practice and more ways to deal with the challenges that confront us continually' (Hillier 2005: 20).

Now – teach yourself!

Whatever the circumstances you face, whatever the type of hangover you experience, you always have a choice about how to interpret them – and it's not always based on logic or careful thought. You can develop your own coping strategies by finding out what others do, by reading books such as this or talking to other people. I started this 'teach yourself' book with a quote from Frank McCourt's memoir of teaching in New York high schools – so I'll finish with one:

You know your role, if the little buggers piss you off from time to time, suffer, man, suffer. No one is forcing you to stay in this miserable underpaid profession and there's nothing to keep you from going through that door to the shimmering world of powerful men, beautiful women, cocktail parties uptown, satin sheets. (McCourt 2005: 152)

It's your choice. You always have a choice. It's up to you. Oh, decisions, decisions . . .

References

Argyris, C. and Schon, D. (1974) *Theory in Practice: Increasing Professional Effectiveness*. San Francisco: Jossey Bass.

Armitage, A., Bryant, R., Dunhill, R., Hayes, D., Hudson, A., Kent, J., Lawes, S. and Remwick, M. (2003) *Teaching and Training in Post-Compulsory Education* (2nd edn). Buckingham: Open University Press.

Atkinson, T. and Claxton, G. (eds) (2000) *The Intuitive Practitioner: on the value of not always knowing what one is doing*. Buckingham: Open University Press.

Ausubel, D., Novak, J. and Hanesian, H. (1978) *Educational Psychology: A Cognitive View*. New York: Holt, Rinehart & Winston.

Bandura, A. (1977) *Social Learning Theory*. New York: General Learning Press.

Boud, D. (ed.) (1988) *Developing Student Autonomy in Learning* (2nd edn). London: Kogan Page.

Brown, J., Collins, A. and Duguid, S. (1989) Situated cognition and the culture of learning, *Educational Researcher* 18(1): 32–42.

Bruner, J. (1966) *Towards a Theory of Instruction*. Cambridge, MA: Harvard University Press.

—— (1977) *The Process of Education*. Cambridge, MA: Harvard University Press.

Child, D. (1997) *Psychology and the Teacher*. New York: Holt, Rinehart & Winston.

Curry, O. (2006) *The Bravo Evolution Report*. London: London School of Economics.

Dantzer, C., Wardle, J., Fuller, R., Pampalone, S. and Steptoe, A. (2006) International study of heavy drinking, *Journal of American College of Health* 55(2): 83–9.

Eysenck, H. (1973) *Eysenck on Extroversion*. New York: Crosby, Lockwood Staples.

Gherardi, S., Nicolini, D. and Odella, F. (1998) Towards a social understanding of how people learn in organisations: the notion of a situated curriculum, *Management Learning* 29(3): 273–85.

Harris, J. (1999) *A Gestalt Approach to Teaching and Learning*. Manchester: Manchester Gestalt Centre.

Heron, J. (1989) *The Facilitator's Handbook*. London: Kogan Page.

Hillier, Y., and Jameson, J. (2003) *Empowering Researchers in Further Education*, London: Trentham Books.

Hillier, Y. (2005) *Reflective Teaching in Further and Adult Education* (2nd edn). London: Continuum.

Hillier, Y., and Jameson, J. (2006) *Managing Ragged-Trousered Philanthropy*, Learning and Skills Development Agency Research Report, Ref. No. 052298. London: LSDA.

Huczynski, A. and Buchanan, D. (2001) *Organizational Behaviour: An Introductory Text* (4th edn). London: Prentice Hall.

Jarvis, P. (1997) *Adult and Continuing Education: theory and practice* (2nd edn). London: Routledge.

Kohler, W. (1925) *The Mentality of Apes*. New York: Harcourt, Brace & World.

—— (1947) *Gestalt Psychology*. New York: Liveright.

Kolb, D. (1984) *Experiential Learning: Experience as a Source of Learning and Development*. Englewood Hills, NJ: Prentice Hall.

Lave, J. and Wenger, E. (1991) *Situated Learning: Legitimate Peripheral Participation*. Cambridge: Cambridge University Press.

Maslow, A. (1942) A theory of human motivation, *Psychological Review* 50: 370–96.

—— (1970) *Motivation and Personality*. New York: Harper & Row.

McCourt, F. (2005) *Teacher Man: A Memoir*. London: Harper Perennial.

Minton, D. (2005) *Teaching Skills in Further and Adult Education* (3rd edn). London: Thomson.

Moore, A. (2000) *Teaching and Learning: Pedagogy, Curriculum and Culture*. London: Routledge Falmer.

Rogers, A. (1996) *Teaching Adults* (2nd edn). Buckingham: Open University Press.

—— (2002) *Teaching Adults* (3rd edn). Maidenhead: Open University Press.

Rogers, C. (1974) *On Becoming a Person*. London: Constable.

—— (1983) *Freedom to learn for the 80s*. Columbus, OH: Merrill.

Schumaker, E. (1977) *A Guide for the Perplexed*. London: Abacus.

Sedgwick, F. (2005) *How to Teach with a Hangover*. London: Continuum.

Sharpe, T. (2005) *Wilt in Nowhere*. London: Arrow.

Thomas, K. (1976) Conflict and conflict management in M. Dunnette (ed.) *Handbook of Industrial and Organisational Psychology*. Chicago: Rand McNally.

Turner, D. (2004) *Theory of Education*. London: Continuum.

Vygotsky, L. (1978) *Mind in Society*, Cambridge, MA: Harvard University Press.

Index